TOWNSEND THORESEN

John F. Hendy

FERRIES
Around Britain

LONDON

IAN ALLAN LTD

Contents

Acknowledgements
The author expresses his warm thanks and appreciation to:
Ron Adams, J. Birse (Caledonian MacBrayne), R. Brown (Highland Regional Council), Len Campbell (Clyde Port Authority), R. G. Clarke (Hovertravel Ltd), John Collins, Miles Cowsill, B. G. Curzon (North Sea Ferries), Richard Danielson, A. Dunlop Munro (Clyde Marine Motoring Co.), Ian Hall, Tom Hamilton, J. R. Haworth (Western Isles Islands Council), J. Holmes (King Harry Steam Ferry Co.), Jane Larcombe (P&O Ferries), Chris Marrow (Viking Island Ferries), J. Mather (Torpoint Ferry), Alastair McRobb, Ann Miller (Tyne & Wear Transport), The Orkney Islands Shipping Co, Paul Ovington (European Ferries), David Parsons, A. Speet (Norfolk Line), Nick Stevens (Sealink UK), Anne Telfer (Western Ferries), Iain Tulloch and Graham Wrightson (Fred Olsen Line).

First published 1985

ISBN 0 7110 1503 1

Published by Ian Allan Ltd, Shepperton, Surrey; and printed by Ian Allan Printing Ltd at their works at Coombelands in Runnymede, England

Bibliography
British Nationalised Shipping – Clegg & Styring (David & Charles)
Island Lifeline – Chappell (Stephenson & Sons)
West Highland Steamers – Duckworth & Langmuir (Stephenson & Sons)
West Country Passenger Steamers – Farr (Stephenson & Sons)
West Coast Steamers – Duckworth & Langmuir (Stephenson & Sons)
Faithfully Yours 'Manxman' – Danielson & Hendy (Stephenson & Sons)
The Denny List – Lyon (National Maritime Museum)
This is Dover & Folkestone – Hendy (Ian Allan Ltd)
Ships of the Fleet – McCrorie (Caledonian MacBrayne)
'Caledonian Princess' – The ship that became Dover's last steamer – Hendy
100 years of Parkeston Quay and its ships – Cone
Car Ferries from Great Britain & Ireland – Widdows
Trip Out 1983/84 – Hamer

Sea Breezes – the magazine of ships and the sea
Cruising Monthly – the newsletter of the Coastal Cruising Association

Cover:
The Isle of Man Steam Packet's new *Mona's Isle* arriving at Douglas from Heysham on 21 April 1985. *Richard Danielson*

Dedication: To Stella

Preface

It is always said that there is no such thing as an up-to-date map, and the task of writing an up-to-date book about ferries has proved almost as difficult to produce. This photographic review was assembled during 1984 and it could well be that by the date of publication, some of the ships contained herein will have been withdrawn from service while others may possibly be engaged upon different routes. The British ferry scene is constantly changing and the privatisation of Sealink UK Ltd, during July 1984 should see long-term alterations within its large fleet.

Ever since I was a ferry-mad schoolboy in Dover, I have longed for the publication of a good photographic album on the subject. Although the academics amongst us may well frown at a book of this nature, the majority will welcome it not only as a guide to short-sea passenger ships but also as a book with which they can relax as they sit beside their warm fire sides during long winter evenings, dreaming of days to come.

When one draws up a list of the ferries around Britain, and here I include the Channel Islands, the Isle of Man and Ulster, it is quite amazing to discover just how many there are – far more than my photographs can portray. It therefore follows that some ferries have had to be omitted, and whereas I have included all the larger ships which serve our shores, it has been impossible to offer a definitive account of all the small ones, some of which offer a seasonal service and double as excursion vessels. However, the small ferry has not been forgotten completely and where possible I have included a sample of these so that the reader can see for himself the variety and multiplicity of ferries to be found within our islands.

The design of our larger ferries has changed considerably since the end of World War 2. There are today but a few ships of this type without the capacity to carry cars and lorries; the ships have become more box-like, and almost gone are the long, lean lines which characterised the prewar ships. Interior fittings too reflect the 'throw-away' society in which we live, with all shades of plastic and formica having replaced wooden panels.

Many readers will regret this sadly inevitable change and so I have included a small selection of historical views showing some of the vessels of yesteryear. Comparisons will of course be made but it will be noted that most of these fine ships enjoyed long careers which were not dictated to by the demands of the roll on-roll off industry. Today any ferry approaching 20 years is regarded as old

although it must be said that the timetable demands of our modern ships are far more excessive than those prior to 1939.

Whereas in those days there were very few independent operators and most Continental and Irish Sea services were operated by the 'big four' British railway companies, today there are few routes which do not feel the pinch of competition. This is particularly so on the English Channel routes where Sealink – British Ferries, SNCF (France) and RMT (Belgium) competes with Townsend-Thoresen, Hoverspeed, Brittany Ferries, Sally Line and Olau Line in addition to a number of purely freight operators.

This competition has brought about bright new liveries with hulls containing the owner's names so that the ships look like vast advertisement hoardings. The last well-known company to succumb to this trend was the Isle of Man Steam Packet Co which retained its smart livery from the founding in 1830 until 1983 when it decided to opt for the free publicity that the name along the hulls of its ships would give. Even Caledonian MacBrayne, the State-owned operator of ferries on the Clyde and Western Isles, has at the time of writing chosen to add its name to most units within the fleet.

Although the numbers of ships have increased over the years – particularly on cross Channel routes – the smaller esturial craft have hit upon hard times. With the general improvement of road communications and motorways since the early 1960s, many of our larger estuaries are now spanned by bridges, resulting in the end of many old ferry services. The Clyde at Erskine, the Forth at Queensferry, the Tay at Dundee, Loch Leven at Ballachulish, Milford Haven at Neyland, the Beauly Firth at Inverness, the Severn and the Humber have all lost their ferries and the list does not end there, The Mersey has just managed to retain hers in spite of fierce competition with road and rail tunnels, but on the Thames, the Tilbury to Gravesend ferry has made increasing losses since the opening of the Dartford tunnel upstream.

In England's West Country, a number of small esturial ferries still exist, linking road systems which have to cross those flooded 'finger' valleys of the Dart, Tamar, Fowey and Fal. Up on the deep fjorded coastline of the West of Scotland there is also a place for the occasional short-cut across the narrows, but even as I write this, the new bridge at Kylesku in northwest Sutherland has just opened, bringing about the end of yet another small but important ferry service.

We may eventually see a Channel Tunnel or bridges linking mainland Britain with the Isle of Wight or the Isle of Skye, but until that distant time, the ferries will reign triumphant.

Within the ranks of the shipping enthusiast, ferries have become more popular in recent years. With so many cheap day-trips now available and the run down of our excursion ship fleets, the switch of interest has been a natural one. Excursion ships were always so popular because people always *chose* to sail in them, either on holiday or in order to see parts of our superb coastline which otherwise would have been difficult to visit. Ferries on the other hand were simply a means to an end. Before air travel became popular, people *had* to travel in them to link up with the great European expresses drawn up on the quaysides on the other side of the Channel. For many, the Channel crossing was the most unpleasant part of the journey: there was always the risk of sea sickness, and they were glad when it was all over.

In other parts of Britain, the ferry was (and in many cases still is) a lifeline to small island communities. In order to bring food and general provisions, the ferry *must* run, and if during the season interested sightseers come along then there are the beginnings of a tourist industry with home-made crafts providing an extra income. Today, Caledonian-MacBrayne's 'Hebridean Highways' provide a reliability, regularity and accessibility which in most cases has changed forever the island communities which its ships serve.

Below:
Boxing Day at Dover in 1983. Here at the Eastern Docks (from right to left and in a clockwise direction) are the *Pride of Free Enterprise, Herald of Free Enterprise, Free Enterprise VIII, N.F. Tiger, Lion, European Enterprise, European Clearway, N.F. Panther, European Trader, Free Enterprise VII, St Christopher* and *Free Enterprise VI.* Where else in Britain could one see such a sight? *John F. Hendy*

Being an island nation, it is impossible for us to turn our backs upon the sea and ships, and with the once numerous fleets of sea-going excursion ships now sadly depleted and numbering just one, the cross-Channel, island or esturial ferry has provided a simple means of getting afloat. Duty-free concessions on the former have of course attracted many, but for the vast majority of Britons the type of ship as seen within these covers will be the only type of ship they will ever, or can ever afford to, sail in. Many would like the chance of a cruise in the 'QE2', but a deck chair behind the funnel of the local ferry at least allows them the chance to dream!

The growth of interest over the years is reflected in the response I receive from writing my monthly article, 'Ferry Scene', in *'Sea Breezes'* magazine. Ever since this feature started in January 1976, I have been able to correspond with and meet people from all around our coasts who share a common interest. In compiling a book of this nature, these contacts have been invaluable, especially as there are parts of our islands that I have yet to visit, and so my special thanks go to all those friends who have, in many cases, taken photographs especially for this book.

I became interested in ferries at an early age but was at an advantage in that the family home was Dover. Without doubt, the port's unique position ensures that it is the 'Mecca' for anyone interested in the subject. During the peak summer season there is always something on the move and there is never time to be bored. At other ports, eg Fishguard, there are mostly two sailings a day throughout the year, but each and every ferry port has its role to play, whether large or small, whether with double-deck link-spans or single slipway; all add to the rich and varied scene which the *Ferries around Britain* provide.

July 1984

John F. Hendy
25 Corner Farm Road,
Staplehurst, Kent,
TN12 0PJ.

London to Newhaven

The Thames

Left:
Since the opening of the Dartford Tunnel in 1964, Sealink's ferry service across the Thames from Tilbury to Gravesend has suffered a dramatic loss of patronage so that today it is a highly uneconomic route to operate. Three similar vessels were built by J. Samuel White at East Cowes for entry into service during 1960/61 but six years later the *Rose* moved to Scotland where she became Caledonian MacBrayne's *Keppel*. Today the *Catherine* is spare, while the *Edith* maintains the link, and the latter is seen here arriving at Gravesend in February 1980, while in the background, on the Essex bank, is Tilbury Riverside station. Further up river, the GLC's Woolwich free ferry provides the important London Inner Ring Road crossing of the Thames. At the time of writing, Sealink British Ferries was attempting to rid itself of its loss-making service and the first refusal is to be given to the local ferry manager and his staff. There are plans to replace the *Edith* with a smaller vessel and switch her to the Solent area.
John F. Hendy

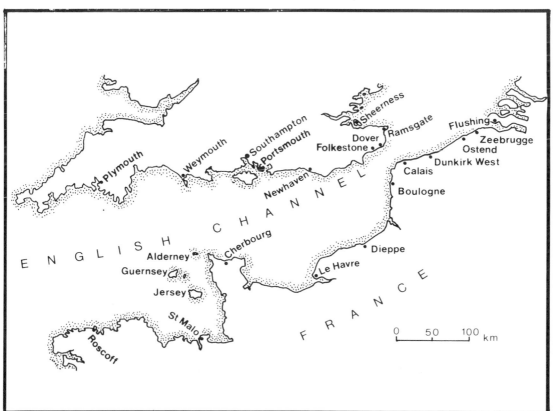

Above:
Olau Line's German-owned super-ferries *Olau Hollandia* and *Olau Britannia* (of 1981/82) maintain the Sheerness to Flushing link providing liner-like standards for 1,600 passengers on the 7½-hour service. Their passenger cabins are all situated forwards while the after-end is given over to the public rooms. Originally owned by Danish shipowner Ole Lauritzen (hence Olau), the line became part of the West German TT-Saga Line empire in 1980. Olau had opened the route in November 1974 and introduced its first passenger/car ferry in January of the following year.   *Olau Line*

Below:
The size of the present ships can be appreciated from this view looking aft from the bridge of the *Olau Hollandia* in July 1983.   *John F. Hendy*

Ramsgate

The Ramsgate–Dunkirk West route is one of our more recent cross-Channel links. It was opened in 1980 by Ole Lauritzen (founder of the Olau Line) with his second-hand former Mediterranean ferry *Nuits St Georges* (ex-*Fred Scamaroni*). The ship was not a success, having no bow-thrust and requiring a tug to berth her, and following the French fishermen's dispute that year she was seized by creditors at Flushing, to where she had been operating while Dunkirk West was blocked.

Below:
The Finnish-owned Sally Line took over the service in 1981 using *The Viking* (ex-*Viking 5*) and since then a number of well-known Scandinavian ferries have been used on the 2½-hour passage. Here is the original *The Viking* alongside at Dunkirk West in October 1982. For the 1983 season she was returned to the Baltic becoming the *Sally Express* before her sale to the Fred Olsen Line in May 1984 and the further renaming of *Bolette*.   *John F. Hendy*

Above:
Taking her place came a new *The Viking* (formerly the Danish ferry *Kalle III*, built in 1974) which is seen here entering the French port in late June 1984. The following month she was joined by the similar Yugoslavian vessel *Njegos* (ex-*Travemunde*) and during the summer of 1984 they operated the route between them. By this time Sally Line had established a firm foothold on Ramsgate and was in the process of extending and enlarging its facilities there, hoping to attract more shippers to the expanding terminal.   *John F. Hendy*

Below:
Sally's second ship for 1985 was none other than the *Sun Express,* their former *Viking 6,* which had surprisingly been bought back from the Sol Line of Cyprus to whom she had been sold in 1982. She is seen here refitting at Chatham prior to entering service in April. Two months later she was again renamed *Viking 6.   Miles Cowsill*

Dover

By far the busiest ferry port in Britain, Dover is the home for ships of British Ferries, SNCF and RMT (trading as Sealink), Townsend-Thoresen and Hoverspeed.

Bottom:
During 1984 most units of the Sealink UK fleet were running in the standard post-1964 livery but without the British Rail arrow markings on their funnels – this in readiness for privatisation of the company in July.

Below:
Here, coming astern out of Calais in February 1985 the *St Anselm* is about to set off on yet another 90 minute dash to Dover while her sistership *St Christopher* is observed nearing her home port in June 1984. In order to give them a separate identity the 'Christopher' had her forward bulwark painted blue and her masts became a darker grey. The addition to the accommodation, aft, was added during their refits back at their builders, Harland & Wolff of Belfast, in 1983.
both John F. Hendy

Above left:
On board the *St Christopher* in Calais and showing the ample deck space and splendid all-round views available to this class of vessel. The twin funnels are a common feature in many of today's modern ferries and allow them uncluttered vehicle decks without the inconvenience of engine room uptakes running up through the centre line of the ship. *John F. Hendy*

Left:
While the *St Anselm* and the *St Christopher* were back in Belfast receiving the extensions to their passenger accommodation, their Holyhead–Dun Laoghaire sister *St David* came south to substitute. Here she is entering Calais on her first call; detail differences should be noted between all three ships. Although primarily engaged on the summer Holyhead services,

the *St David* has also seen employment at Stranraer and Fishguard but in March 1985 she transferred to Dover and took up service to Ostend. Two large, new ships are expected to enter service during 1987, when it is thought that the *St David* may well move again, this time to the Stranraer station. *John F. Hendy*

Above:
Heading away from Calais is SNCF's oldest car ferry, the 1966-built *Chantilly*. At 3,400 gross tons, her size and accommodation do not meet the modern requirements of the Dover Strait routes but due to the late arrival of the *Champs Elysees* in 1984, she was required to cover her Calais–Dover schedules. Although originally a stern only loader, she was converted to drive-through in 1976. *John F. Hendy*

Top:
The 8,479 gross ton *Cote d'Azur* is the third French ferry to be so named and until the arrival of the *Champs Elysees* in the autumn of 1984 she was by far the largest of Dover Strait vehicle ferries. This view shows that although most modern vessels of this type have to be functional, they need not necessarily suffer from a lack of pleasing design. *John F. Hendy*

Above:
SNCF's *Champs Elysees* finally arrived in service in early October 1984 and she is seen here speeding into Dover just four days later. Although basically similar to the *Cote d'Azur*, there are a number of modifications both inside and out (eg a slimmer funnel, no stern docking bridge and larger panoramic windows in her superstructure) and her passenger certificate is for 1,800. During 1985 she reinstated crossings from Dover to Boulogne, and as if to emphasise that she is not a Calais ship, her port of registry is unusually Nantes. *John F. Hendy*

Right:
After her replacement on the Newhaven–Dieppe route, the *Villandry* was sent to Calais to lay-up where she became the relief ship following the sale of the *Compiegne* to Greek owners in 1981. She quickly found employment and saw service at Stranraer, Holyhead and on the Heysham–Douglas (Isle of Man) routes. Her sister ship *Valencay* continued as spare ship at Dieppe running several cruises to and from Rouen during 1984. Like the *Chantilly,* they were converted to drive-through operations having been built as stern loaders in 1965, joining the *Falaise* on the newly opened Dieppe–Newhaven car ferry link. In the autumn of 1984 the *Villandry* was sold to Agapitos Bros of Piraeus after her previous sale to Red Sea owners had proved unfruitful. *John F. Hendy*

Below:
By far the oldest cross-Channel ferry in operation is the French train ferry *Saint-Germain* which entered service as long ago as July 1951. The only major alteration since then has been the building of an additional passenger lounge on top of her promenade deck car garage (aft), but her wooden panelling and general accommodation are pointers to a more elegant age of (Danish) shipbuilding. Although she was expected to be withdrawn from service in 1981, an extensive overhaul was said to give her five more years of service. She is seen here leaving Dover in September 1981. In February 1985, the *Saint-Germain* became a freight-only vessel and her passenger numbers were reduced to just 36.
John F. Hendy

Bottom:
The 'Germain's' running partner on the Dover–Dunkirk West train ferry route is the Italian-built *Saint Eloi* which after long delays at her builders finally entered service in March 1975. Her funnel markings are those of the ALA – a former subsidiary of the British Railways Board – and she is named after the patron saint of her home port, Dunkirk.
John F. Hendy

Top:

The Belgian Government fleet operating between Ostend and Dover has long been known for its elegance and beauty although recent trends have tended to veer away from this practice. The oldest ship is the sole remaining passenger-only cross Channel vessel still in operation – the splendid *Prinses Paola* of 1966. Although only used on spasmodic summer outings, her passenger certificate for 1,800 enables her to carry train loads of Continental travellers leaving the vehicle ferries free to concentrate on freight and the accompanied car trade.

Although her days must now be numbered, the 'Paola' remains as a pleasant reminder of the traditional cross-Channel ship which served our shores so faithfully until ousted by the growing numbers of motor cars and lorries. She is seen leaving Ostend and heading out into a grey, misty Channel in July 1983. *John F. Hendy*

Above:

Looking in bad need of a paint brush, the *Prins Philippe* is pictured here arriving at Dover from Ostend in March 1983. She entered service 10 years earlier, being the first Belgian ship to be built with freight in mind and with the drive through principle. Her fixed mezzanine (or upper car) deck means that apart from the *Prinses Paola* she is the least used of the present day Ostend ferries and she may well be offered for sale in the near future. Her sister *Prince Laurent* has a retractable mezzanine deck and is therefore better suited for the carriage of freight. In May 1985, the *Prins Philippe* took up the summer service between Weymouth and Cherbourg, on charter to Sealink British Ferries. *John F. Hendy*

Below:

The *Prins Albert* was the third Belgian ship to be thus named and was also the final building of the trio of modern RMT vehicle ferries. The *Prinses Maria-Esmeralda* and the *Princesse Marie-Christine* entered service in 1975/76 but differ from the 'Albert' in that they are each able to carry extra cars in the space given over to her lower passenger lounge, aft. In order to further boost the freight carrying capacity of the Sealink Ostend link, the superstructure of the first two ships of the class is being raised and an extra vehicle deck is to be fitted. The 'PME' received hers during the first half of 1985 and the 'PMC' a year later.   *John F. Hendy*

Right:

In order to increase the RMT's freight carrying capacity, in March 1982 the company took the Stena Line's *Stena Nautica* on charter for a period of three years. She was one of four sisters built for the charter market, two of which are now operated by Canadian National Marine while the other is Sealink's *St Brendan* at Fishguard. The 'Nautica' had previously been named *Stena Nordica* (three times) and *Hellas* (twice) but in early 1983 the Belgians purchased her outright, naming her *Reine Astrid* after their passenger vessel of the same name (1958–81) which

had become the jetfoil terminal at Dover Western Docks.

She is seen here in July 1983, making her customary slow departure from Ostend and, from this angle, looking a particularly ugly vessel. Her double loading ramps should be noted plus the ship's previous name which was starting to come through the paintwork between her present name and port of registry. During the following winter she was fitted with stabilisers.   *John F. Hendy*

Below right:

Another Stena Line import came in June 1983 when the *Stena Nordica* (ex-*Stena Danica*) began a three-year bareboat charter. She was built in Yugoslavia in 1974 but in order to give her greater capacity she was stretched vertically in 1977. Before entering service for Sealink (RMT) she had a side door cut in her starboard side to enable her to load additionally from the quayside at Ostend; but just to complicate matters, in Spring 1984 she was renamed *Stena Nautica*, continuing to run with an all-white hull. This fine aerial view shows her leaving Dover, and the famous White Cliffs, astern. The port's two original 1953 link-span bridges can be clearly seen above her funnel.   *FotoFlite, by courtesy Sealink UK*

Above left:
In order to provide foot passengers with a high speed England–Belgium link, RMT introduced its two Boeing jetfoils *Princesse Clementine* (seen here on overhaul in Ostend in February 1982) and *Prinses Stephanie* in May and July 1981. The 316-seat craft cross in just 100 minutes and provide the only such service from any British port. Previous attempts to run these highly sophisticated American-built craft from Brighton, Newhaven, London and Liverpool have all ended in failure although this Ostend service, being Government-backed and rail-linked, looks like being successful. *John F. Hendy*

Left:
P&O Normandy Ferries – as it was then styled – entered service from Dover to Boulogne in April 1976 using the car ferry *Lion* which, due to 'the troubles' in Ulster, had been taken off the Ardrossan–Belfast route (for which she was built in 1967). She is seen here entering Dover in June 1981. In January 1985, P&O sold their loss-making Normandy Ferries operations to the European Ferries Group for £12.5 million. The *Lion* briefly saw service on the Portsmouth–Le Havre link before being withdrawn from service and later sold to Greek Cypriot owners. *John F. Hendy*

Above:
The *Lion* was followed into service by the *nf Tiger* (ex-*Kattegat*) and the *nf Panther* (ex-*Djursland*, ex-*Kalle II*) in June 1978 and January 1980. They both originally came from the Danish company Jydsk Faergefart, being constructed at the same Elsinor yard that built the French train ferry *Saint-Germain* and belonging to the same company as the Sally Line's *The Viking* when she was the *Kalle III*. The 'cow-catcher', below the bow-visor, is a feature common to many ferries and enables the link-span at Boulogne to rest upon it when they are berthed bow-in there. *John F. Hendy*

Left:
From 1974 until 1979, Townsend-Thoresen's Dover
fleet consisted of *Free Enterprise I* to *Free Enterprise
VIII*. Today only the final three of the series remain
there on the Zeebrugge services. There are minor
differences between them, and the uprating of
'F.E.VIII's' accommodation at the end of 1983 pointed
towards several further years of service for this
successful class of ferry. They run in conjunction with
the three 'European' class freighters, and the last of
the 'F.E.' series is seen here loading at Dover's
Eastern Docks in June 1983. Note the dent in her bow
visor – always a vulnerable spot. From June 1985 until
February 1986, the *Free Enterprise VI* and then the
'F.E. VII' are to be raised and stretched in order to
increase their freight carrying capacity. The 'F.E. V'
was called back from Portsmouth to cover the period
of their conversions. *John F. Hendy*

Centre left:
The second high speed cross Channel link is provided
by Hoverspeed – a 1981 grouping of the Swedish
company Hoverlloyd and the British Rail subsidiary
Seaspeed. SNCF was originally intending to join the
consortium but its highly unreliable craft failed to
improve on her disappointing record even after
modifications. Hoverspeed was sold to its directors in
early 1984 in order to save more heavy losses from
being made and so the next few years will be make or
break for the new owners. At the time of writing they
were considering ordering new diesel-engined craft –
these alone would save vast amounts on fuel as the
present SRN4's (Mk II and Mk III) use expensive
aviation fuel. In this picture, GH 2006 *The Princess*

Margaret lifts off at Dover for Boulogne on a rainy day
in April 1984.   *John F. Hendy*

The arrival of the 'Spirit' class of cross Channel ferry
from January 1980 brought about a whole new
thinking with regard to the design and practice of this
type of vessel. These 24kt ships can cross from Dover
to Calais in under an hour – although they are
timetabled for 75 minutes – and five round sailings a
day can be fitted in. Although they are very heavy on
fuel, the company claims that the extra revenue
earned from the fifth trip more than compensates for
this. Sadly lacking in outside deck space, they are well
appointed ships and provide excellent service. The
line of superstructure is most unusual but this
enables the lifeboats to be launched from a lower
position thereby making it easier if the ship is listing.
Aeroplane-type chutes are fitted to assist in
passenger evacuation and interestingly the sisters
are colour-coded for recognition purposes.

Bottom left, Below:
Here the *Spirit of Free Enterprise* is seen leaving
Calais in June 1984 with her green-topped bridge with
white ventilators plus a green painted lift-shaft
towards her after end. The 'Herald' displays these
features in white paint and also has the uprights in her
bridge windows painted black, while the 'Pride' –
seen at speed in August 1982 with the original funnel
markings – has a green-topped bridge with orange
ventilators and an orange lift shaft on the starboard
side.   *both John F. Hendy*

Folkestone

Below:
Sealink's Folkestone–Boulogne link is maintained by the three British ferries *Vortigern, Hengist* and *Horsa*. The *Vortigern* is undoubtedly the most versatile of them all as during the winter months she becomes the relief train ferry on the Dover–Dunkirk West route. She was built on the Tyne in 1969 and entered service on the Dover–Boulogne link in late July. Her original role meant switching to the train ferry route during each of her early winters but the conversion of her side-loading garage into an extra passenger lounge in 1978 reflected her diminishing use as a train carrier. Present thinking is that she will continue in service until 1987 but it is known that SNCF has been anxious to acquire her to replace the *Saint-Germain* and her new owner may well have other ideas for her. When new, the *Vortigern* reflected the British Railways Board's new naming policy of resurrecting characters from the Dark Ages – one which has now, thankfully, been dropped. *John F. Hendy*

Right:
The *Hengist* is seen leaving Folkestone for Boulogne in her intermediate livery before Sealink UK unveiled the present colour scheme at the end of March 1984. Both she and her sisterships *Horsa* and Dieppe's *Senlac* were built at the Naval Dockyard at Brest and have all been very successful vessels carrying large numbers of train-connected foot passengers in addition to the usual traffic. *John F. Hendy*

Below right:
Coming astern into Folkestone is the *Horsa* – the first Dover Strait ship to be treated in her owner's new livery. She replaced the Dover–Calais 'Golden Arrow' ship *Invicta* in the local fleet (in August 1972), and although she is occasionally seen at Dover, both she and the *Hengist* were built mainly with Folkestone in mind. With the arrival of the *St David* on the Dover–Ostend service, Folkestone's overnight freight runs to the Belgian port ceased, leaving the three locally-based ships to the Boulogne route. *John F. Hendy*

Below:
Named after the site of the Battle of Hastings in 1066, the *Senlac* entered service on the Dieppe route in 1973 and until 1985 carried her distinctive buff funnel with the Newhaven–Dieppe joint fleet houseflag. The service has lost money in the past and was officially closed in January 1982, a hard-earned reprieve eventually coming after a bitter struggle. During mid-October 1984 British Ferries announced that it was withdrawing from the Dieppe route and that the *Senlac* would be sold to its French partners which would in future operate the route alone. Her last sailing under the British flag was at the end of January 1985 and she commenced her career with SNCF a month later.

In this April 1978 view the *Senlac* is seen occupying the port's single link-span while the preserved paddle steamer *Waverley* pulls away for a cruise to the Isle of Wight during one of her popular South Coast visits. A yacht completes the scene of diesel, steam and sail. *John F. Hendy*

Right:
Like Dover and Folkestone's *Vortigern*, the *Chartres* was built as a multi-purpose passenger, vehicle and train ferry, and it was intended that she should replace the elderly *Saint-Germain* at Dunkirk West on the arrival of the Calais-based *Cote d'Azur* in 1981. However this was not to be as the Dieppe station urgently required new tonnage with a greater ro-ro capacity and so in the spring of 1982, she was switched there. Her rails have since been covered over. Catching the last rays of a setting sun, the *Chartres* is seen entering Newhaven in October 1983. *John F. Hendy*

Below right:
In order to provide yet more ro-ro capacity, SNCF chartered the Brittany Ferries vessel *Cornouailles* during 1984/85. She was built in Norway in 1977 and during her career with the Brittany company was almost exclusively engaged on the Roscoff–Plymouth link. Her passenger certificate for just 500 made her unpopular and she was replaced by the chartered *Benodet*, of which more later. *Miles Cowsill*

2. The Solent Scene

Portsmouth

Below:
The Portsmouth Harbour Ferry Co operates the sister ships *Portsmouth Queen* and *Gosport Queen* across the narrow neck of the harbour. Both were built at Southampton in 1966 and were notable additions to the fleet in that they had an extra deck. Each also had a totally enclosed deck. The Portsmouth–Ryde passenger ferry *Southsea* lies alongside Portsmouth Harbour station, while on the right the former Portsmouth–Fishbourne car ferry *Caedmon* is off service at the Sealink lay-by berth. *John F. Hendy*

As with both the Portsmouth–Gosport ferries, the *Southsea* and *Brading* were launched on the same day, immediately after each other. These two ships came from the famous Dumbarton yard of William Denny & Bros in 1948, being joined three years later by a similar vessel, *Shanklin*. Following engine troubles, the *Shanklin* was sold to the Firth of Clyde Steam Packet Co, becoming its *Prince Ivanhoe* and operating in association with the preserved paddle steamer *Waverley*. Her career under new ownership was, alas, all too brief and she was wrecked off the Gower coast in August 1981. Meanwhile her older 'sisters' continued to provide a reliable and important service, linking train services at Portsmouth and Ryde. With the privatisation of Sealink UK in July 1984, British Ferries announced that the two remaining passenger ships would be replaced by modern, fast ferries, but it is hoped that one of them will be rescued for excursion work and follow in the wake of the *Shanklin*.

Right:
This photograph shows the *Brading* about to enter Portsmouth Harbour and passing the war memorial on Southsea front. It was taken from the top deck of the new car ferry *St Catherine* which provided a grandstand view of the older ship. *John F. Hendy*

Below right:
Arriving at Ryde Pier Head in the twilight of her career, the *Brading* makes an interesting picture. Being the less reliable of the twins, she is due to be withdrawn from service in spring 1986 while her sister *Southsea* will be refurbished in the Edwardian style and used as a relief and cruising vessel. *John F. Hendy*

Left:
Going astern from berth 6 at Ryde Pier is the Blue Funnel excursion boat *Princessa* built by Camper and Nicholson in 1921 for the local Port of Portsmouth Floating Bridge Co. She is now the oldest of the excursion vessels in the Solent region although many former Gosport ferries still exist in similar roles on the Thames. The *Princessa* is now usually engaged on dock cruises at Southampton allowing the more modern Blue Funnel units to work further afield.
John F. Hendy

Below:
From 1961 until 1983 the sister ships *Camber Queen* (left) and *Fishbourne* were the mainstay of the Portsmouth–Fishbourne car ferry service. During their careers, traffic on the route grew by leaps and bounds so that at the end they were totally inadequate for the route. This unusual photograph shows them together at the Fishbourne link-span in early September 1983 after one of the newer units had gone off service with engine troubles and the laid-up *Fishbourne* was brought back into service for a few days. The 'Queen' was later sold to Portugal and after sale to a local scrapyard, the *Fishbourne* was quickly resold to a Cypriot concern. *John F. Hendy*

Right:
Built at Lowestoft to supplement the services offered by the 1961 twins, the *Cuthred* entered service in 1969 and will be replaced when a third 'St Catherine' class ferry enters service. Although still a double-ender, her passenger accommodation covered the entire width of the vehicle deck and her lifeboats were unusually placed in recessess in her superstructure. Following the 'Dark Ages' trend at the time, the vessel was given the name *Cuthred* and she is seen here setting out from Fishbourne on her 40 minute run to Portsmouth. She is now the reserve vessel. *John F. Hendy*

There can be fewer more attractive sitings for a ferry terminal than that in Fishbourne creek on the Isle of Wight. The *St Catherine* is seen berthed there two months after entering service and it will be noted that, unlike the previous ferries built for the route, she has an easily recognisable bow and stern. Up to 142 cars and 1,000 passengers can be carried in excellent accommodation. The *St Catherine* (named after the headland at the southern tip of the island) entered service without the BR funnel arrows and was the first Sealink ship to appear thus.   *John F. Hendy*

Below:
This splendid shot shows the new Isle of Wight 'Super ferries' *St Helen* (nearest the camera) and *St Catherine* passing in the Solent and wearing the new Sealink UK livery which they received in April 1984. Notice that the further ship does not have the small cowls behind the funnel.   *Sealink UK*

Above:
During the 1983 summer season Sealink experimented with its chartered side-walled hovercraft, GH 2094 *Ryde Rapide*, which it used on the Ryde–Clarence Pier (Southsea) service and on the Ryde–Portsmouth commuter link. Spring 1986 is due to see the introduction of the first of the Australian-built 470 seater catamarans on the Portsmouth–Ryde route, replacing the *Brading* and relegating the *Southsea* to secondary status. *John F. Hendy*

Below:
Fast ferries have existed on the Isle of Wight routes for several years but during 1982, Hovertravel Ltd – the operator of the Southsea to Ryde link – introduced its new AP1-88 craft which use marine technology and diesel fuel and are therefore cheaper to operate than the SRN6s which they replaced. This trials photo of GH 2087 was taken before it was named *Tenacity*; the sister craft is called *Resolution*.
British Hovercraft Corporation

Above:
Since 1976 Portsmouth has also become a
Continental ferry port used today by Brittany Ferries
(for the Saint Malo service and to Caen from June
1986), Townsend-Thoresen (for Cherbourg and Le
Havre), Sealink British Ferries (for Cherbourg and the
Channel Islands) and Channel Island Ferries.

Townsend-Thoresen's extra ship for the summer
service has been the *Free Enterprise V* which moved
down Channel from Dover for the 1982 season
replacing the 'F.E. III' which operated in 1981, which in
turn had replaced the 'F.E. II' which worked the route
in 1980. Following her 1983 season, the 'F.E. V'
received an extensive facelift to her accommodation
and here makes a splendid sight as she nears
Portsmouth in the previous
September.   *John F. Hendy*

Above right:
The Aalborg-built sisters *Viking Valiant* and *Viking
Venturer* are both registered in Southampton and
reflect their original use on the former Thoresen
services from that port to Cherbourg and Le Havre.
Once Portsmouth was opened to Continental traffic,
Southampton was gradually downgraded with the
'Super-Vikings' closing the passenger services from

the end of 1983. They are an extremely popular pair
and as can be seen in this photograph of the
'Venturer' leaving for Cherbourg in July 1984,
excellent outside deck space is a notable feature. A
new 'Club lounge', replacing cabins, was fitted in both
ships during the winter of 1983/84 and this has further
improved the excellent facilties on board. During
1986, both sisters are to have an extra vehicle deck
inserted in order to boost their freight
capacity.   *Miles Cowsill*

Right:
The Brittany Ferries vessel *Armorique* was built in
1972 as the *Terje Vigen* for the Norwegian Da-No Line
and operated a service between Oslo and Aarhus. Her
sale to the French company in 1975 was followed in
1976 with the opening of the Portsmouth–Saint Malo
link on which she operated until 1978 when she was
switched to the Plymouth–Santander and Cork–
Roscoff routes. Following the arrival of the *Quiberon*,
the *Armorique* came back to the Saint Malo station
running in tandem with the *Prince of Brittany*. The
Armorique is seen leaving Portsmouth on her
morning crossing with the Isle of Wight in the
background and the Sealink passenger ferry *Brading*
coming in from Ryde.   *Miles Cowsill*

Above left:
The *Prince of Brittany* started life in 1970 as the Swedish Lion Ferry AB's *Prince of Fundy* on the route between Yarmouth (Nova Scotia) and Portland (Maine). Eight years later she was taken on charter by Brittany Ferries and proved so popular that in 1980 she was purchased outright and registered under the French flag. She is seen here arriving off Portsmouth in the new company livery in March 1984 having left her home port some nine hours previously.
Miles Cowsill

Above:
The *Prince of Brittany* off Southsea beach on the eve of Royal Wedding Day in July 1981.   *John F. Hendy*

Left:
Sealink started its new service from Portsmouth to the Channel Islands in October 1977 using the *Earl Godwin* until the *Earl William* arrived, but she was replaced in March 1981 by the eight-year old *Earl Granville* (ex-*Viking 4* of the Finnish Sally Line). She was one of a series of similar vessels built by Jos Meyer of Papenburg, West Germany – others included the *Viking 5* (Ramsgate's first *The Viking*) and Brittany Ferries' *Corbiere* (ex-*Apollo*). In the summer of 1983 the 'Granville' commenced operating a weekend switch with Weymouth's *Earl William* which involved sailing from there to Cherbourg and to the Channel Isles. Here she is entering Portsmouth during her first season as a British-flag ship and being chased home by the *Prince of Brittany*.   *John F. Hendy*

Left:

The *Earl William* – seen here leaving St Helier, Jersey, in August 1980 – was built in Norway in 1964 as Thoresen Car Ferries' *Viking II*, serving the newly opened routes between Southampton and Cherbourg/Le Havre (routes which British Railways had abandoned in the previous year). After Thoresen's merger with Townsend and with new ships available for the Southampton services, the *Viking II* and *Viking III* spent much of their later careers with the company involved in the charter trade. The *Viking II* was eventually sold in 1977 and after modifications at Holyhead, she took up the Portsmouth–Channel Isles route in January 1978 being eventually replaced there by the *Earl Granville* and consequently moving to Weymouth to in turn replace the turbine steamer *Caledonian Princess*.

In a complete and thorough reorganisation of Sealink's Channel Islands operations, the *Earl Granville* and *Earl William* had £3 million spent on them and commenced the 'Starliner' service in April 1985, carrying just 400 passengers in luxurious surroundings which British Ferries public relations described as the 'Orient Express of the sea'. Calls at Cherbourg have been interwoven with the Guernsey and Jersey routes but with this highly priced service facing competition from Channel Island Ferries, doubts were being expressed as to the long-term viability of the British Ferries gamble. If their service fails to attract the customers, then it is possible that one or both vessels will be switched to a projected new service linking Venice, Istanbul and Kusadasi in Southern Turkey.   *John F. Hendy*

Below left:

A ship with a very full career, the *Benodet* started life in 1970 as the *Apollo* of the Viking Line consortium running between Sweden and Finland. Five years later she was sold to the Olau Line becoming its *Olau*

Kent until along with Mr Lauritzen's other ship (Ramsgate–Dunkirk West's *Nuits St Georges*) she was arrested at Flushing in 1980 over the non-payment of debts. The following year she was again sold to a Danish company which renamed her *Gelting Nord* for use in the Kattegat. Here she was involved in another financial crisis and was chartered to Brittany Ferries as the *Benodet*, commencing service in April 1984 for use on the Roscoff route. In March 1985 she was switched to the Portsmouth, Jersey, Guernsey link of the newly-formed Channel Island Ferries (in which Brittany Ferries holds a 27% share) and as the *Corbiere* commenced a day time alternative to the Sealink 'Starliner' service. With accommodation for 800 passengers and a much less expensive fare structure, CIF was confidently expecting to quickly capture 20% of the market.
Channel Island Ferries

Below:

P&O Normandy Ferries entered service in 1967 on the Southampton–Le Havre route with its white-hulled *Dragon* which was later followed by the French SAGA's *Leopard*. Originally the British-owned vessel was operated by the P&O subsidiary company, the General Steam Navigation Co, but the restructuring of the parent company in 1976 saw the birth of P&O Ferries and two years later the transfer of the *Leopard* to British ownership, although she retains her French crew and registry.

The *Dragon* and the *Leopard* have seen their best years in service and during 1984 remained based on Southampton until labour problems in November finally forced them to switch to Portsmouth where they shared the Brittany Ferries berth. Along with the three Dover ships, these twins were absorbed into the Townsend-Thoresen fleet in January 1985 – the *Dragon* being immediately relegated to seasonal service.   *Townsend Thoresen*

Southampton

The Southampton, Isle of Wight and South of England Royal Mail Steam Packet Co is usually abbreviated to Red Funnel Services and is today the operator of the Southampton–Cowes/East Cowes ferry in addition to operating a local tug fleet.

Below:
The hydrofoils *Shearwater 3,4,5 and 6* provide a fast ferry service between Southampton and Cowes although only two of them are ever on service together. They each carry 67 passengers and were introduced between 1972 and 1982 cutting down the hour-long trip by conventional ferry to just 20 minutes. Here the *Shearwater 3* nears Southampton Royal Pier in September 1977. *John F. Hendy*

Top right:
In August 1979 the oldest of the three Red Funnel car ferries, the 1965-built *Cowes Castle*, is seen entering the River Medina at Cowes. She was originally a bow and side only loader but was sent to Rotterdam at the end of 1975 for lengthening and conversion to drive-through operations. She uses her stern door at Southampton, side doors at Cowes and the bow-ramp at East Cowes. *John F. Hendy*

Centre right:
The *Norris Castle* (of 1968) was also stretched and altered in Rotterdam but reappeared with her main mast forwards of her funnel when she arrived back in Southampton in March 1976. The conversion of the two 'Castles' eventually allowed Red Funnel to dispose of the earlier *Osborne Castle* as their car capacity was raised from about 35 to 75. The 'Norris' is seen here during Cowes Week in 1980 at the start of another Southampton run. *John F. Hendy*

Bottom right:
The third, and largest, Red Funnel ferry is the *Netley Castle* which finally entered service during June 1974 after her builder, Ryton Marine of Wallsend, went bankrupt during her fitting out and she was seized by the company's creditors. She was towed to Southampton and finally completed by the local shipyard, Vosper Thornycroft. Red Funnel's first double-ender proved such a success that her two earlier consorts were converted to drive through operation. On their return, the new Southampton ramp and passenger access walkway did not fit the 'Netley' and during 1976 she required modifications to her Southampton end (when gates were substituted for her fold-down ramp) and access doors were cut into her saloon deck. She is seen here in May 1984 loading for Cowes. *John F. Hendy*

Below:
The *Hotspur IV* was built at the Rowhedge Ironworks in Colchester in 1946 and has maintained the link between Southampton and Hythe across Southampton Water ever since. She is seen here in May 1984 finishing her annual overhaul at her owner's mud berth at Hythe. Beyond, the pier, along which an ancient narrow gauge railway operates, stretches out into Southampton Water.
John F. Hendy

Bottom:
General Estates' two other Hythe-based vessels are seen in this view. The *Hythe Hotspur* is usually used as the cruise boat, running as far afield as Ryde and Southsea but her higher freeboard and sturdier construction see her often on the ferry service at peak times and in rough weather. She was built in 1974 as the Portsmouth Harbour Ferry Co's *Southsea Queen*, passing to the Hythe company some four years later for £160,000. Astern of her in this view is the latest vessel, *New Forester*, coming in from Southampton. Although rather an unattractive vessel, the Littlehampton-built craft provides good covered accommodation and an excellent panorama of the local shipping scene. *John F. Hendy*

Lymington

Below:
The Lymington–Yarmouth service, across the Western Solent, is today operated by the three identical sisters, *Caedmon, Cenwulf* and *Cenred*, which were delivered from the Robb Caledon shipyard at Dundee in 1973. As mentioned earlier, the first of the trio was associated with the Portsmouth route until her transfer at the end of 1983. The sisters are improved versions of Portsmouth's *Cuthred* and side-doors in their superstructure enable them to load foot-passengers directly into their accommodation rather than via the vehicle deck. The *Cenwulf* was the first Sealink British Ferries unit to appear in the full corporate company livery following the de-nationalisation of Sealink UK Ltd in summer 1984. She is seen here on passage during October.
Sealink UK.

Right:
Until the arrival of the *Caedmon*, the third Lymington ship was the 1959-built *Freshwater* – the largest ship on the route when she was built but dwarfed by the later vessels. This picture was taken in August 1979 from the *Cenwulf* and shows the *Freshwater* heading down river towards Yarmouth after vacating the Lymington link-span and moving out of the main channel to allow the incoming ferry to pass. The old slipway is seen astern of her and Lymington Pier station and its single line to Brockenhurst can also be observed. She was fitted with side doors in 1978 in order that she might see relief duty on the Humber between Hull and New Holland the following January in place of her one time Lymington companion, the *Farringford*. She also did this in 1980 but the opening of the Humber Bridge and the consequent closure of the ferry in June 1981 put an end to this. After her 1983 season, the *Freshwater* was sold to a Portsmouth-based scrapyard.   *John F. Hendy*

3. Weymouth and the West via the Channel Islands

Weymouth

Below:
After the withdrawal of the turbine steamer *Maid of Kent* on the seasonal Weymouth–Cherbourg link in 1981, the Venice-built *Ailsa Princess* was transferred from the Stranraer–Larne route to replace her. She entered service in July 1971 but since moving south her role has also included that of the winter relief ship for other routes and this photograph shows her leaving Calais for Folkestone in April 1984. Following the total reorganisation of Sealink's Channel Island services, the *Ailsa Princess* was switched to run in tandem with *Earl Godwin* and for this purpose was renamed *Earl Harold.*   John F. Hendy

The Weymouth–Channel Islands route is perhaps the most difficult of all Sealink's services. Due to operating restrictions, particulary at Jersey, only ferries of a certain size can be used and yet the islands are more popular than ever for the summer tourist trade and the ships frequently sail up to their certificate capacity. However, in the winter months they can sail almost empty.

Right:
The *Earl Godwin* was built as the *Svea Drott* in 1966, being employed on the Helsingborg–Travemunde link. Following the failure of the islands' first car ferry – the turbine steamer *Falaise* – in August 1974, the Swedish ferry was quickly called in and so impressed were her charterers that her purchase followed and she was renamed *Earl Godwin*, taking up station in January 1976. Until placed on the new Sunliner service in 1985 she was associated with the early afternoon departure from Weymouth, and is seen here moving forwards off the port's link-span before going astern out of the harbour during the summer of 1983.
Miles Cowsill

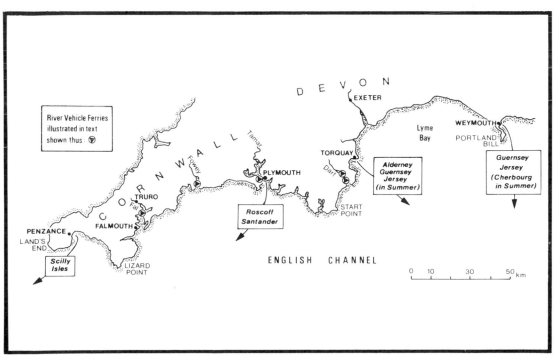

Channel Islands

Top:
Both St Peter Port and St Helier harbours are kept busy during the summer with a constant stream of arrivals and departures of small ferries and excursion boats to and from the other islands or from France.

Here in the Albert Harbour at St Helier in August 1981 are the *Earl Granville* (left), the *Belle de Jersey* (ex-*Emsland*) from Granville, the *Jaguar* from Saint Malo and Emeraude Ferries Saint Malo–St Helier car ferry *Solidor* built in 1965 as the Danish ferry *Langeland* and transferred to this route in July 1977. She carries 40 cars and 500 passengers and crosses in

2½ hours. Both she and the *Earl Granville* were built by Meyer of Papenburg, West Germany.
John F. Hendy

Above:
The *Belle de Dinard* (ex-*Karmsund*) is an early type of Westermarin catamaran and was built in Norway in 1972. Four years later she came to Saint Malo under the ownership of Vedettes Blanches et Vertes maintaining the 90-minute fast ferry crossing to Jersey with the occasional trip to Guernsey. *John F. Hendy*

Above:
Seen here entering St Helier on her first crossing in March 1983 comes the new *Trident* – a very modern Westermarin type. Her arrival sent the *Belle de Dinard* across to work the secondary Granville route while the older and slower *Belle de Jersey* was laid up. *Kevin Le Scelleur*

Below:
This photograph shows just how small is the entrance to St Helier harbour at Jersey. Elizabeth Castle stands out into St Aubin's Bay as the Guernsey-based

Condor hydrofoil *Condor 5* arrives from Saint Malo. The company is a subsidiary of Commodore Shipping which operates cargo services to the islands. Its hydrofoils also serve Alderney and Sark (where passengers are tendered to by launch). The *Condor 5* was built in 1976 and carries 180 passengers. A new hydrofoil is due in service for 1985. *John F. Hendy*

Lack of space does not permit the inclusion of other small ferry/excursion services, most of which operate on a seasonal basis within the Channel Islands.

The West

With the English Channel here at its widest, the only cross Channel services operated from this area are the Brittany Ferries routes to Roscoff and Santander and the Torbay Seaways service from Torquay to Alderney, Guernsey and Jersey. Further west we shall meet the *Scillonian III* but all other ferry services are operated by small vessels which include a series of interesting double-ended vehicle ferries – or floating bridges – used to cross a series of deep, drowned river valleys (or rias) which cause problems to east-west communications in South Devon and Cornwall. Needless to say, these beautiful finger inlets are home for a large number of excursion vessels some of which often double-up as ferries as the need arises.

Torquay

Below:
The *Clansman* was originally one of a trio of car ferries built at Aberdeen in 1964 for services in the Western Highlands. Originally associated with the seasonal Mallaig–Armadale (Skye) link, she was also seen on a number of other routes from time to time. At the end of 1972 she was sent to Troon for lengthening and conversion to drive-through operations for the then fairly new service linking Ullapool and Stornoway (Lewis), but she was not a success and was replaced by the *Suilven* in the following year. However she always went back to Ullapool each winter to run during the *Suilven's* overhaul and also deputised for P&O Ferries *St Ola* on the Pentland Firth link. The *Clansman's* employment during her last 10 years under the CalMac banner was mainly as the Ardrossan–Brodick (Arran) ferry until with the introduction of the new *Isle of Arran* in April 1984, she was laid up and advertised for sale.

She came South to Torbay Seaways in August and is seen here laid up at Philip's yard on the Dart expecting new engines for her 1985 service from Torquay to Jersey and Guernsey. However, problems beset the company as the local council later refused it permission to build a link-span at Torquay and consideration was then given to either operating from Plymouth or purchasing a hydrofoil instead.

In the event, Torbay Seaways purchased the hydrofoil *Springeren* from Danish owners and the *Clansman* was passed to Mira Shipping of Malta. *Brian Maxted*

The Dart

Below:
The Lower Dart Ferry is operated by two 'vessels', owned by the South Hams District Council, one of which is seen here being propelled across from Kingswear to Dartmouth by the launch *Hauley IV*. Having backed her float away from the slipway, the 'Hauley' unties her stern rope and swings herself round on the bow rope so that she is then facing the right way. The other float can be seen above the motor cyclist in the centre-left of the picture.
Richard Danielson

Bottom:
Further up the River Dart is the Higher Dart Ferry built and operated by Philip & Sons of Dartmouth. The present vessel dates from 1960 and is propelled by diesel-electric driven paddle wheels being guided across the fast flowing river by a steel cable. On disembarkation, vehicles cross the preserved Torbay Steam Railway and the line can be clearly seen in this picture. When a train is due, it follows that the ferry is held up until the crossing gates are reopened *Richard Danielson*

Below:
The Kingswear–Dartmouth passenger ferry is operated by Dart Pleasure Craft's *Adrian Gilbert* which entered service in June 1957. Both she and her sister *Humphrey Gilbert* were built at Bideford for British Railways but when the service lost money they were sold to local owners and then to the St Mawes Ferry Co. However, at the age of 20, British Rail purchased them back and spent some £44,000 on refurbishing them in order that they might operate the Tilbury–Gravesend ferry and help to reduce the operating costs on this loss-making service. Unfortunately, permission from the Department of Trade was not forthcoming as they did not offer enough protection for passengers on the exposed lower Thames and so, amidst a few red faces, they were once more put on the sale market. For the 'Adrian' it meant a return home and she is seen here leaving Dartmouth in June 1981.   *Richard Clammer*

Bottom:
The last paddle steamer to operate on the Dart was the 1924-built *Kingswear Castle*. After her long 41-year career on the river she was sold to the Paddle Steamer Preservation Society which eventually towed her to the Medway Marina and began the long process of rebuilding. Years of hard work were rewarded in November 1983 when she set off on trials. Here she is paddling away from Strood Pier (with Rochester Cathedral astern) and serving as a magnificent testimony to the traditional British esturial excursion steamer.   *A. J. Beardsell*

The Tamar

Below:
The year-round Stonehouse to Cremyll ferry service is run by the Millbrook Steamboat and Trading Co with its *Northern Belle*, which was built locally as long ago as 1929. *Richard Danielson*

Bottom:
The same company operates the *Edgcumbe Belle* (ex-*Humphrey Gilbert*) which is often used for relief Stonehouse–Cremyll sailings but is seen here in June 1981 at Mayflower Steps in Plymouth when working the Drake's Island ferry service. *Richard Clammer*

Top:
The Torpoint Ferry is three identical chain ferries which link Devonport with Torpoint in Cornwall. The origins of the route date from 1791 although the first chain ferry was not built until 1843. As in other rivers, the tidal flow in the Tamar is too great to allow a boat to travel directly across, hence the chains to assist them to keep the correct course. Cornwall County Council took over the operation of the link in 1922 and the three present floating bridges date from 1960, 1961 and 1968, having been built at Southampton. From 1961 Plymouth City Council took over joint responsibility for the ferry operation and that of the new Tamar bridge further upstream.   *Torpoint Ferry*

Above:
The *Quiberon* was built for a subsidiary of Swedish State Railways in 1975 as the *Nils Dacke* and operated on a service between Malmo and Travemunde with

her sistership (of different owner) *Gustav Vasa*. In 1982 she was chartered by Brittany Ferries and extra cabins were fitted for use in her new role on the Plymouth–Santander and Roscoff–Plymouth/Cork routes. She has been an extremely popular addition to the Brittany Ferries fleet and in August 1984 the company took up its option to purchase her.
Gordon Bellman Ltd.

Brittany Ferries' two former Scandivanian ferries operate from Millbay Docks at Plymouth. In the autumn of 1984 Associated British Ports announced plans to spend £4million to develop and expand the area and the ferry company has indicated that when the improved facilities are ready in 1986, it will be either stretching the existing vessel or seeking to replace the *Quiberon* with something in the region of 15,000 gross tons.

Below:

Following the *Benodet's* transfer to Channel Island Ferries, Brittany Ferries took the Yugoslav ferry *Njegos* on a two year charter (with an option to purchase) to cover the Roscoff–Plymouth route. Renamed *Tregastel*, she commenced service in April 1985 having been engaged on Sally Line's Ramsgate–Dunkirk West route in the previous summer. She was however no stranger to the Brittany company, having briefly been chartered for the Saint Malo–Portsmouth link before taking up her Sally workings. She was built as the *Travemunde* in 1971 and originally worked the Travemunde (West Germany) to Gedser (Denmark) route before being sold to Yugoslavia 10 years later. *Gordon Bellman Ltd.*

The Fowey

Below:

The Fowey–Bodinnick ferry is operated by C. Toms & Son and consists of two simple floats each propelled by small double-ended motor launches. The present route is a diagonal one and about eight cars and 50 passengers can be carried. *Richard Danielson*

The Fal

Below:
The King Harry Steam Ferry Co operates the chain ferry *King Harry Ferry* which came into service in April 1974 from Penryn builders. Prior to this vessel, a former Saltash floating bridge was used, but, apart from one week in the year when she is slipped, the present 28-vehicle ferry maintains a valuable and very reliable service. It is powered by two sets of Ford diesel hydraulic power units although one is usually sufficient to drive her. Fuel is taken on twice a year! *Richard Danielson*

Scilly

Right:
The Isles of Scilly Steamship Co introduced its *Scillonian III* in May 1977 on the Penzance–St Mary's route. She was built at Appledore in Devon and has a capacity for 600 passengers. Although her gross tonnage is just 1,255, she crosses some of the most exposed waters around our coasts and her high bow and sturdy hull reflect this. The ship is one of the few remaining ferries without a drive-on facility; here she is alongside at St Mary's unloading a furniture lorry. Next to her is the company's inter-islands launch *Tean* (built 1941) which will run ferry passengers out to the other inhabited islands of the group. *Tean* has been known to run to the mainland when required. *Richard Danielson*

4. Irish Sea, Isle of Man and the Mersey

Pembroke Dock

The British & Irish Steam Packet Co's *Innisfallen* was built at Cork in 1969 as its *Leinster*. She was originally engaged on the Dublin route, but in 1980 was switched to Pembroke Dock–Cork and was renamed *Innisfallen* after the sale of the previous ship of that name to Mediterranean buyers and to free her own name for the new ship the building in Cork. Early in 1982, the Rosslare and Cork services were given to one ship and amidst howls of protest the latter route was axed as from February of the following year. Political pressures forced B+I to reintroduce a summer Cork working using the chartered Finnish ferry *Fennia*, but poor advertising saw the company's involvement with the Cork route end once and for all with the termination of the charter in September 1983.

Below:
The photographs show the *Innisfallen* outward bound from Pembroke Dock in April 1984 while the chartered *Fennia* arrives from Cork on her first crossing in June 1983. B+I is hoping to replace the *Innisfallen* with a larger ship. Early in 1985, Sealink British Ferries and B+I entered into a joint pooling agreement whereby they would in future share the revenue on both the Rosslare and Holyhead routes. Whether or not B+I continue to operate their southern service after 1985, remains to be seen.
Miles Cowsill

Fishguard

Below:
In March 1979 Sealink UK took the *Stena Normandica* on a 19-month charter prior to the introduction of the new *St David* on the Fishguard–Rosslare passage.

Although a mechanical defect saw her off service for much of that first season, the 'Stena' proved to be so popular that the company extended the charter for a further five years and switched the *St David* to Holyhead. Much money was spent on modernising the chartered ship and a change of registry from Gothenburg to Nassau in Spring 1984 preceded her change of livery into the new Sealink UK colours. She is seen here at Fishguard in June 1984. In April 1985, Sealink finally purchased the vessel and in the following month, renamed her *St Brendan*.
Miles Cowsill

Holyhead

Below:
Moving north to Holyhead, the Sealink ferry *St Columba* has maintained the Dun Laoghaire route since entering service in May 1977. Her size allowed the company to replace two passenger vessels and a car ferry, but she has been plagued with numerous mechanical problems and her replacements have found it difficult to cope – ideally, two ships are required to cover her.

At 7,836 gross tons she is by far the largest vessel in use on any Irish Sea route and her capacity for 2,241 passengers and 323 cars is impressive. During the winter of 1982/83 she became a one-class ship although she still boasts a 'Pullman Lounge' in which passengers pay a fare supplement. With the de-nationalisation of the Sealink UK fleet in July 1984, her new owner announced that he would seek larger tonnage for the Dun Laoghaire route. *Sealink UK*

Isle of Man

Above:
A vintage Isle of Man scene showing the Battery Pier, Douglas in 1955 with the veteran steamer *Victoria* (of 1907) alongside with the *Mona's Queen* (of 1946) outside her. The *Victoria* was originally built for the South Eastern & Chatham Railways' Dover Strait services before passing to the Isle of Man 21 years later. This view shows her one year before her disposal while the 'Queen' was sold to the Chandris Line in 1962. The Steam Packet passenger fleet numbered nine in 1955 – today it operates just four passenger/car ferries. *Henry Maxwell*

Below:
The company's final passenger-only ship was the *Manxman* of 1955 which remained in service until the end of the 1982 season, by which time she was Britain's last operational passenger-only, turbine cross-Channel steamer. She is seen here in July of that year taking day excursionists home to Llandudno – a service that died with her passing. She was a splendid vessel and being the last of the line it was only right that she should be preserved. Unfortunately her presence in the Albert Edward Dock at Preston has been anything but happy and there are fears for her long-term future.
John F. Hendy

Above:
Leaving the Edward Pier at Douglas for an afternoon sailing to Liverpool is the Steam Packet's first car ferry, the *Manx Maid* of 1962. Her steam bow-thrust is hard at work and as the setting sun catches her, we can reflect upon her splendid lines – the hall-mark of all the traditional Isle of Man ships. The 'Maid' had capacity for 1,400 passengers and 80 cars.
John F. Hendy

Right:
Like her sistership, the *Ben-my-Chree* (of 1966) latterly saw seasonal work although she was the winter relief ship when the two diesels went for annual overhaul. These twin turbine car ferries were the last such vessels in service around our shores and as such they deserve a special place in the story of the ferries around Britain.

The 'Ben' is seen here during her 1983 season when for the first time the company introduced its name along the black hulls of its ships. As can be seen, it was hardly noticeable from a distance and so in 1984 a larger, Mk II, version was applied. This remarkable view shows the turbine working up to 20kt on a Douglas–Liverpool departure when she proved beyond all doubt that she really was a steamer!
Richard Danielson

56

Above:
Competition on the Manx routes ended on April 1 1985 when Sealink Manx Line and the Steam Packet merged with the latter company taking a 60% share in the reorganised company which turned to Heysham for its year-round link.

After some teething troubles, the new *Mona's Isle* entered this service on April 21 running in tandem with the *Manx Viking*. Here she is, newly arrived in Douglas and greeted by mist and rain.   *Richard Danielson.*

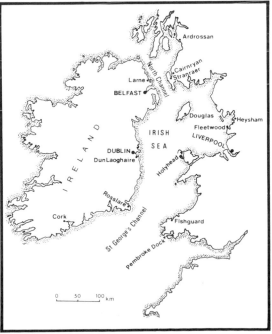

Below:
In May 1980, the Victoria Pier at Douglas was visited by the Fred Olsen/Bergen Line ferry/cruise ship *Venus* – the largest passenger vessel ever to dock there. As can be seen, she completely dwarfed the *Mona's Queen* which had entered service some eight years previously as the Steam Packet's first diesel car ferry.   *Richard Danielson*

Right:
The Isle of Man Steam Packet's *Lady of Mann* is seen here approaching Douglas during June 1984 with the new application of the company's name in 7ft high letters along her hull. Both she and the 'Queen' are side loaders, and no heavy freight is carried. Like her sister, the 'Lady' is a product of the Ailsa yard at Troon, entering service four years after her, in 1976.   *Richard Danielson*

Left:
The Steam Packet's ro-ro ship *Peveril* came to the company via P&O Ferries for which she was the *N.F. Jaguar*. Originally taken on charter, she was then purchased by Barrow ship owners James Fisher & Sons and came to her Douglas registry on a demise charter from them.

She was built in Norway as the Finnish *Holmia* in 1971 but two years later passed to Singapore owners on charter to a West German company for which she operated as the *A.S.D. Meteor*. A further charter saw her under the management of the P&O subsidiary, the Belfast Steamship Co on the joint P&O/Sealink service from Heysham to Belfast. She was eventually purchased outright by P&O, taking the Sealink name *Penda* and operating in the company's livery. Eventually being replaced by larger tonnage, she found her way to Southampton where as the *N.F. Jaguar* she assisted the *Dragon* and the *Leopard* on the Le Havre run. Following that, she was laid up at Liverpool where the Steam Packet took an interest in her, starting its own ro-ro service in the summer of 1981.

This view of the *Peveril* shows her still in P&O colours and stuck in the Mode Wheel Lock of the Manchester Ship Canal in April 1983, prior to being painted in the IoM livery. Following the introduction of the new year-round Heysham service, the *Peveril* was chartered to Belfast Freight Ferries for their Belfast–Heysham link, to which she was no stranger.   *Richard Danielson*

Above:
A sunny summer afternoon in late July 1983 sees Sealink's *Manx Viking* arriving at Douglas from Heysham. She was built for the Spanish Aznar Line as the *Monte Castillo* but was purchased by the Manx Line in 1978. Mechanical problems beset her and she proved to be a most unreliable vessel and it was little surprise when the company fell into financial difficulties. James Fisher & Sons of Barrow in conjunction with Sealink UK baled it out and until the merger of April 1985 the service provided the Steam Packet with its only serious competition since it was founded in 1830.

Due to be renamed *Earl Henry* for the seasonal Weymouth–Cherbourg service, the 'Viking' was retained at Heysham for the 1985 season.   *John F. Hendy*

The Mersey

Of all the estuaries in Britain, the only one to retain its traditional ferry services, in fierce competition with road and rail tunnels, is the Mersey. It was a hard struggle to keep the ferries but the work of local pressure groups now seems to have paid off and the Mersey Passenger Transport Executive appears to recognise that they have a valuable role to play.

Until local government reorganisation, the Mersey ferries were managed by Birkenhead Corporation and Wallasey Corporation, running to Woodside and Seacombe respectively from Liverpool's Pier Head. The routes across this narrowest part of the river are about ¾ mile long but within this narrow neck, the water can be extremely turbulent as the tide rushes into and out of the wider river inland. It can be appreciated that the ferries have to be particularly sturdy craft.

Below:
Seen against a Liverpool skyline, Birkenhead Corporation's ferry steamer *Bidston* operated the Woodside route between 1933 and 1962. She was built locally at Cammell Laird's yard and was one of four similar ships which were gradually replaced from 1958 after the arrival of the first pair of diesel ferries. *George Danielson*

Right:
Birkenhead's *Mountwood* and *Woodchurch* came from Philip & Sons of Dartmouth in April and May 1959. Here the *Mountwood* leaves the Pier Head in April 1980 bound for Seacombe (right – with the *Royal Iris* alongside) churning up the muddy waters of the river as she sets off. Shortly after this photograph was taken, the *Mountwood* had her mainmast removed. *John F. Hendy*

Below right:
The last ship built for the old Birkenhead Corporation fleet was the *Overchurch* which entered service in March 1962 after completion by Cammell Laird. She is seen here in April 1980 crossing from Liverpool to Seacombe and being passed by the B+I jetfoil *Cu-na-Mara*, then on trials before commencing a Dublin service which soon ended in failure.

In preparation for the Festival of Flowers in 1984, the old Birkenhead ships were painted in a special red, white and blue livery and a new service, up river to Otterspool, was opened. *John F. Hendy*

Top:
The only former Wallasey Corporation ferry still in service is the futuristic-looking *Royal Iris* which entered service on the Seacombe link in April 1951. She was a product of Denny's Dumbarton yard and was seen by her designer as a 'maritime bus' producing excellent accommodation for both excursionists and ferry passengers who also enjoyed her on the summer link to New Brighton. Today she is used as a lunch-time restaurant at the Pier Head, although as she is now very much the 'old lady' of the Mersey she cannot be expected to last very much longer.   *John Collins*

Above:
Liverpool is also the English terminal of the B+I twins *Connacht* and *Leinster* which offer night crossings to Dublin and day sailings from Holyhead. They were both built by the Verolme Dockyard at Cork in 1978 and 1981, the *Connacht* being originally associated with the company's southern (Cork) route from Swansea and then from Pembroke Dock in the spring of 1979. She also came to the Pool of London on a flag waving exercise in January 1979. The *Leinster* is seen here during her only spell on the Pembroke Dock–Rosslare route in March 1984. At the end of 1984, B+I was planning to switch its Irish terminal from Dublin to Dun Laoghaire although opposition to this move from Irish transport unions was fierce. The Sealink/B+I pooling arrangement at Holyhead brought about the ending of the fierce competition which both these ferries experienced at the Sealink port where open hostility had marked B+I's arrival.
Richard Danielson

The Belfast–Liverpool route was traditionally the preserve of the Belfast Steamship Co but as its last ships, the *Ulster Queen* and the *Ulster Prince*, became older and uneconomical, P&O withdrew from the route in November 1981.

Below:
Picking up the pieces came the Irish Continental Line's subsidiary, Belfast Car Ferries, which introduced its *Saint Patrick* – renamed *Saint Colum 1* – in May of the following year. She was the ship which had inaugurated the ICL's Rosslare–Le Havre route in 1973 following an earlier withdrawal by P&O Ferries. The Swedish company, Lion Ferry AB was originally involved in restarting the link, and the ship is in fact the sister of Brittany Ferries' *Prince of Brittany*. This stirring photograph was taken from the Steam

Packet's *Ben-my-Chree* as the 'Colum' was outward bound from Liverpool and running into a force 9 gale in February 1984.   *Richard Danielson*

Bottom:
During the *Saint Colum 1's* annual overhaul (or during the odd period of breakdown), the parent Irish Continental Line send the *Saint Patrick II* up from Rosslare. She is seen here in January 1984 at the Belfast Car Ferries berth (formerly used by P&O) on Donegal Quay in the centre of Belfast. The *Saint Patrick II* was built as the *Aurella* for the Finnish SF Line – part of the Viking Line group – but was sold to the Irish in 1982. Both she and the *Saint Killian II* (ex-*Stena Scandinavica*) operate the ICL's Le Havre and Cherbourg routes.   *Rodney MacKenna*

5. Scotland

Stranraer

Sealink's Stranraer–Larne ferry *Antrim Princess* entered service in December 1967 and this unusual photograph shows her at anchor off Gourock nine days before taking up the passage on her arrival from Hawthorn Leslie's Tyneside yards. The Caledonian Steam Packet's small motor vessel *Maid of Skelmorlie* is alongside acting as a tender.
Tom Hamilton collection

Bottom:
The 'Antrim' is seen again approaching Larne in March 1984. Notice how her accommodation has been extended aft, and that in readiness for privatisation her BR arrows have been removed from her funnel. In an early document outlining his intentions for the company, the ship's new owner has intimated that he intends to replace her with more modern tonnage and the 'Antrim' is due to take up the Heysham–Douglas link by February 1986. *Ken Kane*

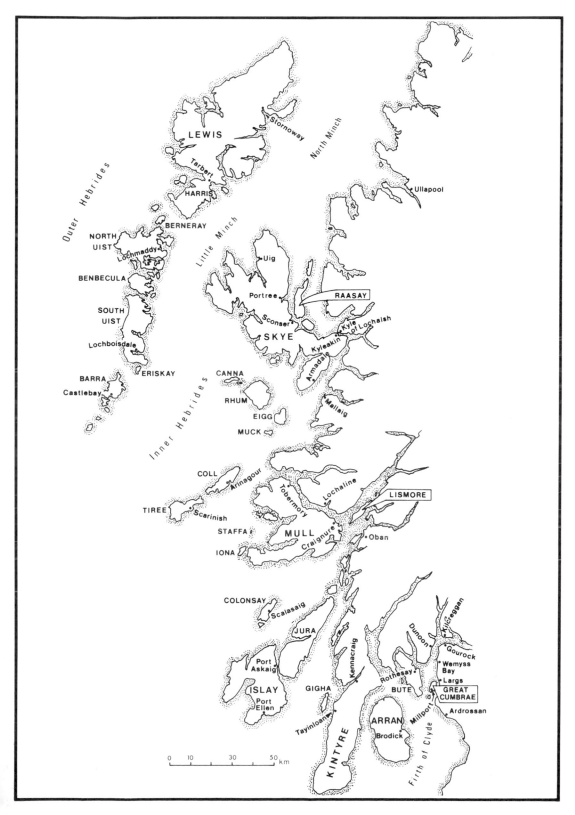

LEWIS

Stornoway

North Minch

Outer Hebrides

Tarbert

HARRIS

Ullapool

BERNERAY

NORTH
UIST

Lochmaddy

Little Minch

Uig

BENBECULA

Portree

RAASAY

SOUTH
UIST

Sconser

Kyle of Lochalsh

Lochboisdale

SKYE

Kyle

Kyleakin

BARRA

ERISKAY

Armadale

Castlebay

Inner Hebrides

CANNA

RHUM

Mallaig

EIGG

MUCK

COLL

Arinagour

Lochaline

LISMORE

TIREE

Scarinish

Tobermory

STAFFA

MULL

Oban

IONA

Craignure

COLONSAY

Scalasaig

JURA

Dunoon

Kilcreggan

Gourock

Port
Askaig

Kennacraig

Rothesay

Wemyss
Bay

Largs

ISLAY

GIGHA

BUTE

GREAT
CUMBRAE

Port
Ellen

Millport

Ardrossan

Tayinloan

KINTYRE

ARRAN

Brodick

Firth of Clyde

0   10   30   50 km

65

Top:
Seen here arriving at Larne is the *Darnia* – yet another Stena Line 'import' having been built in 1977 on the River Danube in Austria as the *Stena Topper*. James Fisher & Sons of Barrow purchased her a year later, renamed her *Darnia* and chartered her to Sealink for the Stranraer station. Following the transfer of the *Ailsa Princess* to Weymouth in 1982, the *Darnia's* passenger certificate was increased from 92 to 412 and here she is in September 1982 showing her new accommodation designed to meet the requirements of her enlarged status. Initially stability was a problem but this type of conversion at least solved the immediate difficulties in which the route could have found itself following the departure of the 'Ailsa'.

It is of interest that one of the *Darnia's* original sisterships, the *Stena Tender*, serves the port of Portsmouth in the form of Townsend-Thoresen's chartered ro-ro vessel *Viking Trader*.
Rodney MacKenna

Above:
The first of Harland & Wolff's new passenger and vehicle ferries for Sealink was the *Galloway Princess* which took up station at Stranraer in May 1980. She is a smaller version of the *St Anselm, St Christopher* and the *St David*, and in order to accommodate her, the buoyed channel in Loch Ryan was deepened and widened at the southern end. She is a notable addition to the Stranraer fleet being the largest ship and the first to offer double-deck loading. In order to fill the vacancy left by the expected departure of the *Antrim Princess*, the Stranraer route was to originally have Folkestone's *Vortigern* but arrangements were being made for chartered tonnage to be used instead. *Ken Kane*

Below:

The rival North Channel route from Cairnryan to Larne is operated by Townsend-Thoresen whose parent company, European Ferries, also owns the Ulster port. After unsuccessful attempts at running passenger/car ferries on the route with the *Free Enterprise III* in 1974 and the *Free Enterprise I* in 1975, the *Free Enterprise IV* was switched there in May 1976 and became a great success and a firm favourite in spite of subsequent attempts by the company to replace her. The 'F.E. IV' is now the oldest of the 'F.E.' series still in operation, having entered service from Dover in June 1969. She is seen here at speed in Loch Ryan, outward for Larne. *Harry Cathcart*

Bottom:

Although at the time of writing the ro-ro vessel *Gaelic Ferry* was serving the Portsmouth—Le Havre route, she is seen here early in 1984 approaching Larne from Cairnryan. Formerly of the Atlantic Steam Navigation Co fleet, she came from Swan Hunter's Tyneside yard in 1963, at first being used on the Tilbury—Antwerp and Rotterdam links, later being switched to Felixstowe. Now one of the oldest ro-ro ships serving our shores, she boasts excellent passenger accommodation for a limited number of lorry drivers. With the take-over of P&O at Portsmouth, the 'Gaelic's' future is now uncertain. *Ken Kane*

Above:
Another former ASN Co ship, the *Europic Ferry*, also came from Swan Hunter four years after the 'Gaelic', being associated in her early years with the Felixstowe–Europort route. Her main claim to fame came during the Falklands conflict when she was one of a number of short-sea vessels called up for active service. Her bright-orange Townsend-Thoresen hull was too visible in San Carlos Water, or 'Bomb Alley' as it became known, and so it was daubed with grey in order to make her look less conspicuous to Argentine bombers. This photograph shows her on arrival back in Southampton in July 1982. During 1984 she was operating the North Channel link with the 'F.E. IV' *Gordon Hammond, by courtesy of Townsend-Thoresen*

The Clyde and Western Isles are the home of Caledonian MacBrayne which claims to sail to 23 Scottish islands. However, it is certainly not the only operator for amongst others, the Strathclyde and Highland Regional Councils and the Western Isles Islands Council also provide small ferries for minor, yet important, crossings. Unfortunately, as with the Channel Islands, it has been impossible to include all ferries and only the larger and more well-known ones are included here.

The Firth of Clyde

Right:
The *Isle of Arran* is Caledonian MacBrayne's latest ferry and is seen here leaving Ardrossan for Brodick (Arran) during her second week in service in April 1984. Her capacity for about 80 cars and 800 passengers (Class III certificate)/446 passengers (Class IIA certificate) should meet all the requirements of the island which she serves and she was the first unit of the fleet to be built with the company name along her hull. Her black paint level was dropped during her first overhaul in order to give her a more balanced look.
David Parsons

Above:
The small island of Great Cumbrae is served in the summer months by the passenger vessel *Keppel* which operates between the island's 'capital', Millport, and Largs. The *Keppel* was originally the *Rose* of the Tilbury–Gravesend ferry but moved northwards in April 1967. The service she now operates has been under threat of closure in recent years and during 1983 the islanders were claiming that they would run the service themselves if CalMac withdrew. Storm damage to Millport Pier during the winter of 1984–85 made the continuation of the route appear unlikely. *Bernard McCall*

Below:
The *Isle of Cumbrae* was named as a result of a competition among schoolchildren in Millport. A car ferry service to the island had been started in March 1972 and increasing traffic brought the new ship into service in April 1977. Her success has been instrumental in the running down of the *Keppel's* service, but for foot passengers, Cumbrae slip is outside Millport and therefore less convenient. Notice the company's funnel painted on the superstructure beneath the wheelhouse. The 'Cumbrae' is seen leaving Largs in April 1984. It is planned to replace this vessel with two 'Super-Island' class ferries in 1986. At that time, it is expected that the *Isle of Cumbrae* will be moved to the Lochaline–Fishnish (Mull) route. *David Parsons*

Right:
Moving northwards to the Isle of Bute, the primary ferry route operates between the 'capital', Rothesay and Wemyss Bay. It was the last Clyde route to be converted to roll on-roll off and the *Saturn* was built at Troon entering service in February 1978. Similar in many respects to the earlier *Jupiter* and *Juno*, her design incorporated a number of modifications, noticeably in the bridge and mainmast areas.

This fine photograph shows her when new using her bow-thrust to push her away from the pier at Rothesay although she no longer advertises the fact that she is the 'Rothesay Ferry'. *Caledonian MacBrayne*

Below left:
The secondary route to Bute is via Colintraive, on the mainland, to Rhubodach across the famous narrows known as the Kyles of Bute. It is operated by two former Kyle of Lochalsh ferries, the *Portree* (seen here arriving at her mainland terminal) and *Broadford* (at anchor offshore). Each ferry carries 10 cars and will probably be replaced by a single new 'Super-Island' class vessel in 1986 or 1987.
Bernard McCall

Below right:
This magnificent period Clyde scene dates from September 1952 and shows the David MacBrayne turbine steamer *King George V* calling at Dunoon en route from Gourock to Ardrishaig, while alongside the pier the Caledonian Steam Packet Co's paddle steamer *Marchioness of Lorne* has called on her way from Craigendoran to the Holy Loch. *John Guy*

Below:
Today's scene at Dunoon shows the ferry *Juno* leaving for Gourock on her regular service during October 1980. Sistership *Jupiter* was first introduced on to the route in March 1974 followed by the *Juno* in December. Although lacking the fine looks of the ships that preceded them, they have proved very popular, and at certain times have appeared elsewhere on the Clyde. Today the *Jupiter* has a particularly easy roster being used as the stand-by vessel and also running the morning Royal Naval Armament Depot sailings from Gourock to Kilcreggan. She is also the relief vessel for Bute and Arran, while the *Juno* continues to be the 'workhorse' on the route for which she was built. *David Parsons*

Top right:
The rival route from the Renfrewshire bank across the Upper Firth to the Cowal peninsular is operated by Western Ferries (Clyde) Ltd, which operates the service from McInroy's Point, near Gourock, to Hunter's Quay, a crossing time of just 20 minutes. The oldest ferry operated is the *Sound of Sanda* built at nearby Dumbarton in 1938 as the Southern Railway's *Lymington* of the Lymington–Yarmouth route. Following the introduction of the larger tonnage in 1973, she was withdrawn and laid up, then being sold and brought back to the Clyde in April 1974. Although then aged 36, the *Sound of Sanda* has given her new

owners more years of faithful service – ample testimony to the way in which she was built and how she is maintained, although she is today used as the relief vessel. *courtesy Western Ferries*

Centre right:
Operating the Western Ferries route with the 'Sanda' are two former Swedish ferries, *Sound of Scarba* (ex-*Olandssund III*) and the *Sound of Shuna* (ex-*Olandssund IV*) built in 1960 and 1962 and made redundant by a new bridge linking the island of Oland to the mainland. They were towed separately across the North Sea and through the Caledonian Canal in March and May 1973, but delays in the building of McInroy's Point terminal meant that the service was not ready until June when the *Sound of Shuna* performed the honours. The *Sound of Scarba's* late arrival meant an hourly schedule until during mid-July she took up station and reduced this to half-hourly. Here the *Sound of Shuna* is seen approaching McInroy's Point in June 1978. *L. Schofield*

Bottom right:
The Renfrew to Yoker diesel-electric chain ferry was operated by the Clyde Port Authority and is seen here approaching Renfrew slip in March 1984, two months before its replacement. The service is now operated by two passenger landing-craft type vessels called *Renfrew Rose* and *Yoker Swan*. *Ian Hall*

Above:
The Clyde Marine Motoring Co runs from its base at Princes Pier, Greenock and operates the ferry service from Gourock to Kilcreggan which is extended to Helensburgh in the summer months. The company is also involved in cruising and amongst its vessels are the *Kenilworth* (built in 1936 as the *Hotspur II* for the

Southampton–Hythe ferry) and *The Second Snark*. This latter vessel was built by Denny's of Dumbarton in 1938 as their yard tender/launch and she is seen here off Strone Point in August 1984 whilst on a charter sailing.
both George Young courtesy of Clyde Marine Motoring Co

Top:
Caledonian MacBrayne introduced its eight small 'Island' class ferries between 1971 and 1976. Each carries about five cars and 50 passengers and all have proved very useful additions to the fleet serving smaller communities in remoter areas of the CalMac system. Pictured at Tayinloan in October 1983, the *Coll* is seen discharging from the island of Gigha (background). Normally served by the *Bruernish*, the service was originally operated from the Islay terminal at nearby Kennacraig in West Loch Tarbert and its introduction saved the Islay boat the inconvenience of calling at Gigha whilst on passage.   *Ian Hall*

Above:
Approaching Kennacraig comes the *Pioneer*, inward bound from Port Ellen in Islay. She entered service in August 1974 but in June 1978 her original mainland terminal at West Loch Tarbert was closed in favour of that used by Western Ferries, further down the loch at Kennacraig. This made manoeuvring far easier and effectively reduced the crossing times to Islay. In May 1979 the *Pioneer* was fitted with large new side lifts to enable her to in future work the summer service across the Sound of Sleat between the railhead of Mallaig and Armadale on the Isle of Skye. The ship is spare during the winter months and is able to relieve other large units of the fleet. This view shows her on a return visit to Kennacraig in October 1983 when she was relieving the regular vessel *Iona*.   *Ian Hall*

Below:
The MacBrayne motorship *Lochiel* at the original West Loch Tarbert pier in June 1952. Another Denny product, she entered service in 1939, but with the growth of vehicle traffic in the 1960s she required modifications to allow her to carry 16 cars – all lifted on of course. Sold out of service in 1970 she became the *Norwest Laird* operating an unsuccessful service between Fleetwood and Douglas, Isle of Man. Laid up at Glasson Dock at the end of that season, she was purchased by Courage three years later and since 1977 has resided in Bristol as a floating pub.
John Guy

Bottom:
Western Ferries also operates the small *Sound of Gigha* across the narrows of the Sound of Islay on a service between Feolin (Jura) and Port Askaig (Islay). Built at Bideford for Eilean Sea Services, she entered service during the summer of 1966 as the *Isle of Gigha* and was involved in a tramping capacity as a modern, lorry-carrying 'puffer'. Her size and the nature of her construction severely limited the scope of her operations and having survived a capsizing in November 1966, she returned to service until her owners were forced into liquidation in February 1968. Purchased by Western Ferries (Argyll) Ltd in the following January, the 65 gross tons vessel took up her present route in March 1969, and today as the *Sound of Gigha* this interesting little ferry (seen here at Feolin) has a passenger certificate for 28.
M. J. Borrowdale

Top:
The car ferry *Glen Sannox* dates from 1957 when she was built for the Arran service. Much has happened during her long career from her conversion to link-span loading in 1970, with spells on the Bute and Cowal services and being re-engined before briefly becoming the Firth of Clyde's cruise ship from 1978. She appeared in the West Highlands on the Oban–Craignure (Mull) service in 1974 and since then has been a regular sight there. It is impossible to do full credit to her in this brief paragraph but during 1984 she was laid up during the summer, seeing winter service back at Oban on the Craignure and Scalasaig (Colonsay) routes. She is seen here alongside at Scalasaig in April 1984 after her 2½-hour crossing from the mainland.   *David Parsons*

Above:
Taken at Port Askaig (Islay) in May 1984, this delightful view shows the regular Islay car ferry *Iona* alongside on arrival from Kennacraig with the *Columba* out in the Sound of Islay on a cruise from Oban. The famous Paps of Jura are prominent on the left of the photograph, as is the new application of the company's name along the hulls of its ships.
Ian Hall

Above:
The *Caledonia* was built in 1966 as the *Stena Baltica*, coming to the Clyde some four years later and earning the claim to fame that she was the first drive-through ferry in the region. She was placed on the Ardrossan–Brodick (Arran) crossing and proved successful, but the limitations of her vehicle deck were against her and she was switched to the Oban–Craignure route in summer 1976 returning to Arran in the winter. The arrival of the new *Isle of Arran* in 1984 has meant that she will in future be spare during the winter months. She is seen here leaving Oban in September 1979.   *David Parsons*

Bottom left:
Although the *Iona* is now associated with the Kennacraig–Islay route, since entering service in May 1970 she has seen a very varied career from the Clyde to Stornoway. She is seen here beneath the ramparts of the stronghold of the MacNeil's of Barra – at Castlebay – in August 1975. When she was first used on this service, her lack of cabins made her an unpopular choice and so during her refit that year she was fitted with extra cabins on her bridge deck, her dummy funnel was removed and her engine room uptakes were both extended by 6ft. Finally replaced in the Oban–Lochboisdale–Castlebay (Outer Isles) route by the *Claymore*, the *Iona* was switched to the Islay service as from February 1979.
M. J. Borrowdale

Top:
Another view of Castlebay, this time in August 1980, with the *Claymore* alongside. She is a product of the Robb Caledon yard at Leith entering service in early 1979 on both the Inner and Outer Isles runs from Oban. She is able to discharge her 47 cars over her stern at both Oban and Lochboisdale (South Uist) but requires her side hoists at all her other ports of call. *David Parsons*

Left:
'Drive on' at Oban's North Pier in 1937. Here, by way of planks, a Riley Merlin is being driven directly on board the David MacBrayne motorship *Lochinvar* before she sails up the Sound of Mull to Tobermory via Lochaline and Salen. It was not until April 1974 that this type of loading became 'official' with the opening of the stern loading link-span. *John Guy*

Above:
Back in the late 1950s Oban's waterfront was a very different place than that seen today, rightly deserving its name of the Charing Cross of the north. Here the Inner Isles mail vessel *Claymore* lies at the Railway Pier (left), as does the Sacred Isles excursion steamer *King George V.* Leaving the North Pier is MacBrayne's *Lochnevis* – dating from 1934 – on a Fort William excursion. *John Guy*

Below:
The Oban–Lismore Island connection is maintained by the 'Island' class vessel *Eigg* – the sixth vessel of the group which entered service in February 1975 and began her association with this route a year later. *David Parsons*

Above:
The car ferry *Columba* was built for the Oban–
Craignure (Mull) service in July 1964. Then, following
her sistership *Clansman's* stretching and conversion
to drive-through for the Stornoway route in 1973, she
was sent north to work her summer Mallaig–
Armadale (Skye) roster. This was to be a brief
association, however, as after the sad withdrawal of
the veteran turbine steamer *King George V* it was the
Columba that was chosen to take her place on the
round Mull, Staffa and Iona cruise in addition to
working the Inner Isles mail run to Coll and Tiree and
also out to Colonsay. During the winter months she
relieved the third ship of the class, the *Hebrides*, at
Uig (Skye). This photograph shows the *Columba* at
her most unusual location – at the lonely outlying
Hebridean island of Hirta in the St Kilda group, some
40 miles west of 'the Long Island'. Two sailings were
operated, in May 1979 and a year later – the latter
commemorating the 50th anniversary of Hirta's
evacuation when the last 36 inhabitants left their
wind-swept island which had been inhabited for

thousands of years. The *Columba* is seen anchored in
Village Bay beneath the cliffs of Oiseval down which
the islanders used to climb in order to gather in the
harvest of sea birds and their eggs.
M. J. Borrowdale

Below:
This highly evocative photograph shows the
McCullum Orme steamer *Dunara Castle* at anchor in
Village Bay, Hirta in August 1934. She was a regular
summer caller there after her entry into service in
June 1875 until World War 2. Even after the island's
evacuation in August 1930, at which she assisted,
tourists and former St Kildans still came back to
witness the wild beauty and the isolation of this
'island on the edge of the world'. The island of Dun is
seen on the left of this view and even though the
houses had only been left for four years when this
picture was taken, the roofs had long since
disappeared.
G. E. Langmuir collection

Above:
The Western Isles Islands Council operates a pair of car ferries which are similar in some respects to Caledonian MacBrayne's 'Island' class ships. Here the *Eilean Na H-Oige* is seen approaching Ludaig (South Uist) in August 1980 after having crossed on the 15-minute run from the island of Eriskay in this, her first year in service. Three years later the sister ferry *Eilean Bhearnaraigh* took up the Newton (North Uist)–Berneray crossing.   *Bernard McCall*

Left:
A really splendid sight as she approaches the North Pier at Oban in August 1952 on an Inner Isles livestock run is the steamer *Hebrides*. She was built in 1898 for McCallum's West Highland trade, making many trips as far afield as St Kilda where she operated with the *Dunara Castle*. She soldiered on until 1955 – by which time she was under the David MacBrayne houseflag – after a remarkable career during which time the pace of life in the Western Isles had changed little. It is impossible to imagine any present day short sea vessel lasting for anywhere near her length of service.   *John Guy*

Top right:
The Highland Regional Council operates the important ferry crossing between Corran and Ardgour across the narrows in Loch Linnhe. With the opening of the bridge across the Beauly Firth (between the Black Isle and Inverness) in 1982, the displaced Kessock ferry *Rosehaugh* was switched to Corran, and after modifications entered service in October. In July 1984 the Unapool–Kylestrome ferry closed with the opening of the new bridge across Kylesku in northwest Sutherland. The *Maid of Glencoul* – built in 1975 – was that crossing's principal vessel and also transferred to Corran. She is seen here on station at Kylesku in September 1983.   *Highland Regional Council*

Above:
The *Lochmor* is based on the West Highland railhead of Mallaig and is primarily used to serve the Small Isles – Rhum, Eigg, Muck and Canna. Her arrival in July 1979 caused some relief as her predecessor had sunk in Mallaig harbour some four months earlier.

When not serving the Small Isles, the *Lochmor* runs up the Sound of Sleat to Kyle of Lochalsh railhead, in summer cruising to Portree, the capital of Skye. She is seen here arriving at Kyle of Lochalsh in August 1980 with the Kyleakin slipway and ferry astern.
Bernard McCall

Above:
The Kyle of Lochalsh to Kyleakin (Skye) ferry service is worked by the sisterships *Kyleakin* (1970) and *Lochalsh* (1971), both of which are capable of carrying 28 cars on the five-minute crossing. Here the *Lochalsh* approaches the mainland terminal in August 1980. *Bernard McCall*

Below:
The last of the 'Island' class ferries was the *Raasay* of 1976, which has spent almost all her career on service to the island whose name she carries. The Skye terminal is at Sconser and the vessel is seen arriving there after crossing the Narrows of Raasay and entering Loch Sligachan. *Bernard McCall*

At the time of writing a replacement ferry for the
Hebrides was being built at Selby. She was the first of
the three sisterships to be built at Aberdeen during
1963/64 and took up station at Uig (Skye) in April 1964
crossing to Tarbert (Harris) and Lochmaddy (North
Uist). Although she has relieved on other routes, the
Hebrides has been a most faithful member of the
Caledonian MacBrayne fleet and is seen here leaving
Tarbert in June 1979.   *David Parsons*

Bottom:
The *Suilven* maintains the service from Ullapool to
Stornoway (Lewis) having been brought off the
stocks from a Norwegian yard to replace the
Clansman in August 1974. She was originally to be
named *Basto VI* for a service across the Oslofjord and
her capacity for 528 passengers and 120 cars makes
her ideal for the 3¼-hour crossing of the Minch. This
photograph shows her on the Clyde after one of her
annual refits during which time the *Clansman*
maintained the route. Following this latter ship's sale
in 1984, the Stornoway relief vessel was the new *Isle
of Arran.*
Caledonian MacBrayne

The Orkney Islands

Below:
The link between the mainland of Scotland across the stormy Pentland Firth to the Orkney Isles is operated by P&O Ferries' *St Ola*. She was built for P&O's subsidiary company the North of Scotland, Orkney & Shetland Shipping Co (known as the 'North Company') in 1975 but a year later transferred her ownership to the parent company. The Scrabster (near Thurso)–Stromness service takes two hours and the 'Ola' has accommodation for 400 passengers and 85 cars. The nature of her crossing can be appreciated by her heavy bow, built to withstand the swells and seas met on the passage. Since this photograph was taken the *St Ola* has had the P&O houseflag painted on her funnels and the company name is now in white on the pale blue portion of the hull.   *P&O Ferries*

Right:

The Orkney Islands Shipping Co's passenger vessel *Orcadia* is its largest ship, having come from the Hall, Russell yard in Aberdeen in June 1962. At 619 gross tons she can carry 281 passengers and a large amount of livestock on her services associated with the northern group of islands. At the time of writing a replacement was being considered. *Orcadia* is seen here alongside Whitehall Pier at Stronsay in October 1981: the photograph captures a typical island scene with much hustle and bustle – a car hanging precariously on the hoist, tractors collecting drums of petrol, a new supply of paraffin in the tank, while out of view there maybe cattle or sheep waiting to be shipped.

Bulk cargoes are handled by the *Islander* which also carries general cargo and passengers (12 only) to the islands of Shapinsay, North Ronaldsay, Rousay, Egilsay and Wyre. The *Orcadia's* usual schedule is from the islands' capital Kirkwall (Mainland) to Eday, Stronsay, Sanday, Papa Westray and Westray on Mondays, Wednesdays (outwards), Thursdays (inwards) and Fridays, although the order of call is varied. On Thursdays she also runs between Kirkwall and Rousay, Egilsay and Wyre while Fridays see a North Ronaldsay trip.   *M. J. Borrowdale*

Bottom left:

Arriving at Stromness in the *St Ola* the Orkney Islands Shipping Co's car ferry *Lyrawa Bay* can be seen. She was originally the Faroese *Sam* and entered service here in September 1976 after modifications carried out at Leith. Originally a crane loader, she is now a drive on vessel using link-spans at Houton (Mainland) and Lyness (Hoy).   *W. Paul Clegg*

Below:

Built for the Isles of Scilly Steamship Co as its *Scillonian*, this ship is now in her fourth life. She was built in 1956 for her owner's service from Penzance to St Mary's, but following the arrival of the new vessel in 1977 she was sold to P. & A. Campbell Ltd for excursion work on the Bristol Channel. Her four-year spell under the company's house-flag as the *Devonia* saw her briefly engaged as a ferry for workers involved in building on oil rig at Loch Kishorn (Wester Ross), and during the summer of 1977 she ran a series of highly unsuccessful Thames excursions.

After Campbell's had ceased operations, in 1981 she was sold to Torbay Seaways and in May 1982 she made her maiden voyage from Torquay to Guernsey. Cars could also be handled on the seven-hour crossing (5¼ hours to Alderney) but by 1983 the company was looking at the possibility of replacing her with a drive on-drive off car ferry, this in spite of opposition from the local council. During the autumn of 1984 Torbay Seaways purchased Caledonian MacBrayne's car ferry *Clansman* and sold the *Devoniun* to Norse Atlantic Ferries which renamed her *Syllingar* (the Norse name for the Scillies) and introduced her on the Kirkwall (Orkney), Pierowall (Westray), Scalloway (Shetland) route in mid-December.   *Viking Island Ferries.*

The Shetland Islands

Below:
The mainland–Shetland link is provided by P&O
Ferries' *St Clair* which in 1984 was given a £2.3million
overhaul in order to give her a further 10 years of
service. The 'Clair' came to the route in 1977 (and was
originally intended to work it for five years) prior to
which she had enjoyed a varied career. She started
life in 1970 as the TT Line's *Peter Pan* running
between Travemunde and Trelleborg. P&O Southern
Ferries then acquired her in 1973 for the company's
Southampton–San Sebastian route where she ran as
the *S.F. Panther*. Unfortunately the service operated
at a loss and two years later she was chartered to the
Da-No Line as the *Terje Vigen* (the previous ship of
that name having become Brittany Ferries'
Armorique) for the Oslo–Aarhus link. She then came
back to the P&O fleet and is seen here in Bressay
Sound on the southbound voyage in May 1984.
Iain Tulloch

Bottom:
Apart from the passenger/vehicle ferry service P&O
also operates the roll on-roll off ships *St Magnus* and
Rof Beaver. The former is seen leaving Lerwick for
Stromness (Orkney) and Aberdeen in April 1984. She
was formerly Poole–Cherbourg's *Dorset*, Belfast
Steamship Co's *Ulster Sportsman* and the *Donautal*,
being built at Bremerhaven in 1970 and coming to the
old North Company routes eight years later.
Iain Tulloch

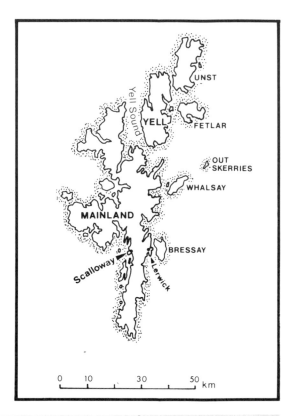

0 10   30   50
km

Below:
The *Rof Beaver* is also a West German-built roll on-roll off vessel, dating from 1971 and gaining her present name five years later after having had five previous names, her first being *Bibiana.* In this photograph she is seen leaving Lerwick for Leith (her usual route) in April 1984. Until 1983 she regularly called at Sullom Voe moving large quantities of plant there for the construction of the new oil terminal.
Iain Tulloch

Bottom:
Between May 1973 and September 1975, the Shetland Islands Council introduced five sisterships for their inter-island routes: Toft (Mainland) to Ulsta (Yell) operated by the *Fivla* and *Thora;* Gutcher (Yell) to Belmont (Unst) and Oddsta (Fetlar) operated by the *Geira;* Laxo (Mainland) to Symbister (Whalsay) operated by the *Fylga;* and Lerwick (Mainland) to Maryfield (Bressay) operated by the *Grima.*

Here the *Thora* is seen approaching Toft pier in April 1984. The sisters carry 10 cars or three commercial vehicles and 93 passengers.
Iain Tulloch

Below:
The first of the quins, the *Fivla*, was sold to Newfoundland in 1983 and was replaced by the larger *Hendra* which was built on the Mersey in 1982. On her arrival, *Hendra* was placed on the Laxo–Symbister route and the *Fylga* was moved in turn to the Yell Sound crossing to work in tandem with the *Thora*. Dogged by mechanical troubles in her early months, the *Hendra's* increased capacity has helped to relieve much summer congestion, and a smaller sister *Fivla* arrived from the Clyde in April 1985 to replace the *Geira.*   *Iain Tulloch*

Bottom:
The *Kjella* of 1957 was a former Norwegian fjord vessel which the SIC purchased in February 1980 for £32,000. Today she acts as the reserve ship but has proved very useful during periods of overhaul and breakdowns. During early 1984 and 1985 she was chartered by the Orkney Islands Shipping Co to serve its south islands during the *Lyrawa Bay's* overhaul. Before entering service she was given a new engine, bulkheads and ramps and allowed the company to operate a year-round two-ferry service on the Yell Sound route.   *Iain Tulloch*

Above:
Pictured here in Lerwick harbour in April 1984, the *Filla* is seen arriving from the Out Skerries – two small islands some 25 miles and two hours sailing to the northeast: their population is about 100 spread out between Housay and Bruray. The new ship was built at Flekkefjord in Norway – bad weather delaying her arrival in Shetland until November 1983. She has on occasion operated to Fair Isle when the *Good Shepherd III* has been off service and at the time of writing a link-span at Bruray was expected to be built. *Iain Tulloch*

Below:
The oil survey/research ship *Aqua Star* is pictured here alongside the Victoria Pier at Lerwick early in 1984. She was originally the North Co's *St Ola* (1951) and is best known for her service on the Pentland Firth route between Stromness and Scrabster until her replacement by the present *St Ola* in January 1975. In her new role she has seen service in the Mediterranean and has even sailed as far as Canada's east coast. The state of her paintwork perhaps points to her prolonged use in exposed water. *Iain Tulloch*

Top:
During the *St Clair's* extensive overhaul in February–
April 1984, P&O Ferries chartered the Faroese car
ferry *Smyril*. She is no stranger to the British ferry
scene having worked a summer service from her
home port of Torshavn to Scrabster since 1976 which
was later extended to include calls in Norway,
Denmark and Iceland. She dates from 1969 when she
was built at Aalborg as the *Morten Mols* for the Mols
Line's internal Danish service. *Iain Tulloch*

Above:
In the spring of 1983, the international services of
Strandfaraskip Landsins were reorganised and a new
company called Smyril Line was formed. The *Smyril*
was retained for internal Faroese services while the
Swedish Lion Ferry AB sold the company its *Gustav
Vasa* – a sister of Brittany Ferries' *Quiberon* – which
was renamed *Norrona* on the termination of its
Travemunde–Malmo service. A similar service to that
operated by the *Smyril* was given in that first season,
but 1984 saw Lerwick substituted for the British call
instead of Scrabster. P&O Ferries markets the service
which calls at Lerwick on Mondays, Bergen (Norway)
on Tuesdays, Lerwick and Torshavn (Faroe Islands)
on Wednesdays, Seydisfjordur (Iceland) on
Thursdays, Torshavn on Fridays, Hanstholm
(Denmark) on Saturdays and Torshavn and Lerwick
again on Mondays. During 1984 sailings were offered
between May and September and this link is the only
continental ferry service operating from a Scottish
port. *Steffen Weirauch*

6. Down the East Coast

The Tyne

Right:
The *Shieldsman* is a double-ended passenger ferry built at Pembroke for the Tyne & Wear Passenger Transport Executive in 1976 for the service between North and South Shields. This diagonal route requires such a vessel in order to shorten the crossings (thereby saving fuel) and to give services of greater frequency at peak times. Her ramps on either side assist with rapid turn round times, the 350 passengers going ashore immediately the ship is berthed.   *courtesy Tyne & Wear Transport*

Below:
The Fred Olsen/Bergen Line sisterships *Venus* and *Jupiter* entered service in 1966 on their routes between Harwich, Newcastle, Amsterdam and Cuxhaven to the Norwegian ports of Stavanger, Bergen, Kristiansand and Oslo. However, during the winter they change identity and become *Black Prince* (seen here) and *Black Watch*, operating cruises to the Canary Islands for Fred Olsen and bringing back vast quantities of tomatoes.

In 1981, the Danish ferry operators DFDS took the sisters on charter and maintained the Tyne–Norway sailings although in 1983 only Stavanger and Bergen were visited. A year later they were used on the Tyne–Esbjerg service but for 1985 the newly-formed

Norway Line (a group of Norwegian tourist firms) has taken the *Jupiter* on a two-year charter, and she will operate between the Tyne and Bergen between mid-May and the end of October. Her sister *Venus* will continue to run on the Esbjerg and Gothenburg routes for DFDS in tandem with the sale-listed *Winston Churchill.*

Both Norwegian ships are now nearing the end of their careers although it looks likely that the *Venus/Black Prince* is to have her passenger accommodation enlarged from 350 to 500 at the expense of her cargo role. In this situation, the *Jupiter/Black Watch* could be sold.   *Fred Olsen Line*

Hull

Below:
Hull is the UK base of North Sea Ferries, a company jointly owned by P&O and the Dutch operators Nedlloyd. The company began its operations in December 1965 with the British flag *Norwave* followed in March 1966 by the Dutch *Norwind* – both then serving the Rotterdam route which the long-established Associated Humber Line (a subsidiary of British Railways) had previously abandoned as a loss-making service. The capacity of the new ships was for 249 passengers and 70 cars, but with the route quickly becoming popular, they were soon shown to be too small. After the arrival of the *Norland* in June 1974, the *Norwave* was switched to the new overnight Zeebrugge route and was followed by her sister with the arrival of the *Norstar* in December.

The *Norwind* is caught by the afternoon sun, as she sits in the Prins Filipsdok at Zeebrugge in November 1983. The following summer the company opened new berths and a passenger terminal in the outer harbour.   *John F. Hendy*

Right:
The *Norland* (British) and *Norstar* (Dutch) took over the King George V Dock, Hull to Europort route in June and December 1974 and have continued to see traffic grow to such a degree that larger ships have been ordered for March 1987. The *Norland* was one of the British ferries involved in the Falklands Task Force, taking the 2nd Battalion of the Parachute Regiment out on the 25-day sailing from Portsmouth. After hostilities had ceased, she served as a prison ship, repatriating captured Argentines to Montevideo (Uraguay) and Puerto Madryn (Argentina). She returned to the Humber with due ceremony in February 1983, but during her absence North Sea Ferries was forced to charter Sally Line's *Viking 6* and then the Irish Continental Line's *Saint Patrick II*.
Bernard McCall

Below right:
The *Wyre Lady*, seen approaching Waddington Lock at Swinton in April 1983, may seem a little out of place in a book of this nature but she boasts an interesting history. She was built in 1938 as the Caledonian Steam Packet's *Ashton* for service on the Clyde. Both she and her sister *Leven* were used at some time on the Gourock–Dunoon, Largs–Millport and Gourock–Holy Loch services before being sold in 1965. The *Ashton* was purchased locally, becoming the *Gourockian* before passing to the Fleetwood–Knott End ferry where she took her present name. Following her spell there, she was moved to the Severn to run excursions before Alan Oliver of Doncaster purchased her to operate on the Sheffield & South Yorkshire Navigation, offering a summer waterbus service and an occasional outing to the Humber.   *Richard Clammer*

Great Yarmouth

The Norfolk Line operates an eight-hour crossing from Great Yarmouth to the Dutch port of Scheveningen using three roll on-roll off vessels. The *Duke of Norfolk* and *Duchess of Holland* each carry 12 lorry drivers, but the 1981-built *Duke of Holland II* carries 36 passengers during the summer months and therefore offers accommodation to accompanied cars on this quietest of routes.   *Norfolk Line*

Felixstowe

Top right:
The European Ferries group subsidiary, the Felixstowe Dock & Railway Co, owns and operates the port of Felixstowe and under its management it has become Britain's number one container port. The only ferry company now operating from the Suffolk port is sister company Townsend Thoresen which has the former Stena Line twins *Nordic Ferry* and *Baltic Ferry* (6,455 gross tons) engaged on the roll on-roll off Europort crossing. Each is capable of carrying 140 lorries and both were called up to see service in the Falklands war. The ships were built in Japan in 1978 as the *Merzario Espania* and *Stena Transporter*, being lengthened in 1981 and 1980 respectively at Bremerhaven.   *Townsend Thoresen*

Above right:
The Felixstowe-Zeebrugge route was started in October 1974 using the Thoresen car ferry *Viking II* (now Sealink's Channel Island ferry *Earl William*), but on her arrival from Denmark she was joined by the second of the 'Super Viking' class of ships, *Viking Valiant*, which worked the route until the *Viking Voyager* entered service in January 1976 (after which time she was transferred to Southampton). The fourth ship of the class, *Viking Viscount*, arrived on station in May 1976 and since then the twins have established the Zeebrugge route as one of the most popular of short-sea crossings, attracting much traffic from the Midlands and the North. Here the 'Viscount' leaves Felixstowe in July 1984.   *Miles Cowsill*

Below:
Crossing the Orwell and Stour estuaries from Felixstowe to Harwich comes the *Brightlingsea*, built in 1925 for the London & North Eastern Railway. She closed the service for British Railways at the end of

1961 but the following year she was purchased by a local concern and amidst great rejoicing in the Haven ports the link was reopened in May. Following the death of the owner in 1979, she was bought by the Felixstowe Dock & Railway Co (a European Ferries subsidiary). The closure of the Butlin's holiday camp at Clacton and the opening of the Orwell bridge at Ipswich badly reduced passenger numbers and during mid-1984 the service and its ship were once again for sale. It is hoped that the 152-passenger *Brightlingsea* will continue in service well beyond her 60th year.   *John F. Hendy*

Above:
The main Harwich–Zeebrugge vessel is the *Speedlink
Vanguard* – yet another Stena Line ship (what would
British ferry operators do without them?) being built
in Holland during 1973 as the *Stena Shipper*. After a
period of charter in New Zealand she was lengthened
and sold to Greece in 1977. When her owner ceased
operations she found her way back to Stena, and in
1980, after a £4million refit on the Tees, she came on a
two-year charter to Sealink UK as the train ferry

Speedlink Vanguard. The original intention was that
she should fill the gap before two new 'jumbo' ferries
were ordered for 1983/85, but when plans for these
ships fell through the 'Vanguard' was required to stay
on. She hit the national headlines in December 1982
when she collided with and sank the Townsend
Thoresen vessel *European Gateway* off Felixstowe.
Her charter is due to end in 1986 and a new ferry is
planned with capacity of up to 75 wagons as opposed
to her own capacity for 46.   *Miles Cowsill*

Left:
The train ferry service from Harwich to Zeebrugge commenced in April 1924 using three identical ships built on the Tyne for the War Department at the end of World War 1. The last ferry built specially for the route was the *Cambridge Ferry*, which arrived on station in January 1963. A service to Dunkirk was operated between 1967–82 but the Harwich train ferry link has undergone considerable change since 1980 and four ships have been replaced by two. During 1984 the 'Cambridge' was only being used four times a week, spending the rest of the time swinging on a buoy in the Stour. The continuation of her boat deck to the stern was added in 1977 to allow her to carry import cars from Zeebrugge. She is seen here in June 1984 shortly after arriving from overhaul and receiving a non-standard new livery which retains the British Rail red funnel and arrows (even though these had previously been painted out), reflecting the fact that the train ferries remain on charter to the British Railways Board. *Miles Cowsill*

Above:
A proud day for Sealink UK on 27 March 1984 when its 17,043 gross tons *St Nicholas* crossed from her annual overhaul in Dunkirk to Dover, where in preparation for privatisation she appeared before the press to unveil the company's new livery. The vessel was built for the Swedish Sessan Line as the second of a pair of sisters, but before completion, Sessan was absorbed by its rivals, the Stena Line. She entered service at the close of 1982 as the *Prinsessan Birgitta* and came to Britain in June 1983 as the Harwich–Hook of Holland route's replacement for the *St Edmund* (sold to the Ministry of Defence) and the *St George*. *John F. Hendy*

Top:
The Hook of Holland route is run jointly between
Sealink partners British Ferries and SMZ. The Dutch
vessel *Prinses Beatrix* is a magnificent example of a
modern-day ferry, having accommodation of a very
high standard whilst fulfilling her requirements as a
car and vehicle ferry. Her arrival in service in June
1978 saw the withdrawal of the route's last
passenger-only ship, the *Koningin Wilhelmina*. Both
the *Zeeland* and *Prinses Beatrix* are due to be
replaced in April 1986 when SMZ introduces a huge
new 30,000 ton ferry with accommodation for 2,100
passengers, 500 cars or a 220-car/80-lorry mix.
Bernard McCall

Top right:
The SMZ ferry *Koningin Juliana* was the company's
first roll-on vessel, coming from Cammell Laird's
Birkenhead yard in 1968. British Rail provided the *St
George* to work with her on the new-look combined
service (previously the Dutch had run the day service
whilst BR sailed by night), but the arrival of larger
tonnage relegated these first car ferries to secondary
status, the *St George* being withdrawn in June 1983,
while the 'Juliana' survived until shortly after the
chartered *Zeeland* arrived in April 1984. This July
1979 view sees the *Koningin Juliana* passing Harwich
on a morning sailing to the Hook, supplementing that
of the *St Edmund*. The 'Juliana' was later sold as an
exhibition ship to promote Dutch exports and for this
new role she was renamed *Tromp*.   *John F. Hendy*

Centre right:
The great drawback of the *Koningin Juliana* was her
limited freight space; a larger vessel was required to
stand in before the arrival of SMZ's answer to the *St
Nicholas*. The ship in question was the Larvik–
Frederikshavn Line's *Peter Wessel* which
commenced charter in April 1984 as the *Zeeland*. Her
greater capacity – 1,500 passengers, 270 cars/26
lorries against the 'Juliana's' 1,200 passengers, 212
cars/13 lorries – reflected Sealink's continued policy
of winning back customers from the rival Olau Line,
which has dominated the market since the arrival of
its large ships in 1981/82.   *Sealink UK*

Bottom right:
From the Town Pier at Harwich in July 1979, the
incoming DFDS flagship *Dana Anglia* is seen entering
the Stour on her arrival from Esbjerg, while in the
distance, on passage from Ipswich to Europort, North
Sea Ferries' ro-ro freighter *Norsky* leaves the Orwell.

The *Dana Anglia* was built in 1978 at a time when
the fortunes of the company were in the ascendency –
the North Sea eventually becoming its own private
'lake' with the take-overs in 1981 of the Tor Line and
Prins Ferries. However, expansion was too quick and
this, coupled with a disastrous attempt at cashing in
on the American cruise market, saw a sudden change
of fortunes for the Danish company and a rapid
contraction following tremendous financial losses.

Another superbly appointed ferry, the Aalborg-
built *Dana Anglia* suffers from being over-funnelled,
and on her visit to the Pool of London, where she was
named in May 1978, the 12ft extension pipes were
removed for fear of interfering with Tower Bridge.
They were soon replaced though, her designers
feeling that without them the downfall of diesel fumes
upon her after decks would inconvenience the
passengers.   *John F. Hendy*

Below:
The former Swedish Tor Line twins *Tor Britannia* and *Tor Scandinavia* originally used Felixstowe as their main British base, but following their take-over by DFDS in 1981 (after a brief merger with the Sessan Line) and the Suffolk port's interest in expanding the container traffic, in April 1983 the ships were switched to Harwich. Until that year they also served Amsterdam, but the reorganisation of the company saw 1984 sailings to Gothenburg and Esbjerg. The 'Tor' twins were built at Lubeck, the 'Britannia' entering service in May 1975 and her sister in the following April. Immingham services were operated until 1978.   *Miles Cowsill*

Bottom:
Prins Ferries operated its *Prinz Oberon* on the Harwich–Bremerhaven link and *Prinz Hamlet* on the Harwich–Hamburg service, but following heavy losses on the former route it was closed in December 1982. Sealink UK briefly chartered the 'Oberon' before the *St Nicholas* entered service and, although for sale, she made a brief reappearance on the summer 1984 Cuxhaven route, also putting in a weekly crossing to Gothenburg. The *Prinz Hamlet* (seen here arriving at Harwich in May 1984) continues to maintain the Hamburg link. She entered service in 1973, originally operating from the Navy Yard at Harwich, but Parkeston Quay was used from May 1979, just as it had been before the switch there 10 years previously.   *Miles Cowsill*

Right:
Although the DFDS charter of the *Jupiter* and *Venus* continued to provide the Fred Olsen Bergen Line with easy summer revenue, their 1984 switch to operate the Danish and Swedish services from the Tyne as well as to Norway prompted Olsen to relaunch his service from Harwich to Kristiansand (last run in 1981) using the 11-year old *Bolero*. The Wednesday afternoon departures between June and August were so well booked that the company intimated that a more intensive service would be given in 1985. In a surprise move, Olsen purchased the *Viking Song* from Rederi AB Sally. Formerly used on the Helsinki–Stockholm service, her new owner has renamed her *Braemar*.   *Fred Olsen Line*

Below right:
A final look at Harwich, Parkeston Quay, illustrating how quickly the British ferry scene can change. In the five years between the taking of this photograph and the writing of this book, the DFDS Esbjerg ferry *Dana Regina* has been transferred to the Copenhagen–Olso route, the Sealink ferry *St George* has been withdrawn from service and sold to Greece, while the same company's 1947-built train ferry *Suffolk Ferry* (far right) has passed for scrapping.

Large scale changes have been promised at Harwich involving the reclaiming of Bathside Bay so that it may one day rival nearby Felixstowe as a top container port.   *John F. Hendy*

Appendix 1

Ships mentioned in the text and presently engaged in service on North Sea, English Channel or Irish Sea routes.

Name (†denotes on charter)	Gross tonnage/Year	Route	Former name(s) (earliest listed first)/ Notes
Belfast Car Ferries (a subsidiary of Irish Continental Line)			
Saint Colum I	5,285/73	Belfast–Liverpool	ex Saint Patrick
B+I			
Connacht	6,812/78	Dublin–Holyhead	
Innisfallen	4,849/69	Rosslare–Pembroke Dock	ex-Leinster
Leinster	6,808/81	Dublin–Liverpool	
Brittany Ferries			
Armorique	5,732/72	Saint Malo–Portsmouth	ex-Terje Vigen
Prince of Brittany	5,475/70	Saint Malo–Portsmouth	ex-Prince of Fundy
Quiberon	7,927/75	Plymouth–Santander/Roscoff Roscoff–Cork	ex-Nils Dacke
Tregastel†	3,999/71	Roscoff–Plymouth	ex-Travemunde/ ex-Njegos
Channel Island Ferries (allied with Brittany Ferries)			
Corbiere†	4,239/70	Portsmouth–Jersey/Guernsey	ex-Apollo/ ex-Olau Kent/ ex-Gelting Nord/ ex-Benodet
DFDS			
Dana Anglia	14,399/78	Esbjerg–Harwich	
Prinz Hamlet	5,830/73	Hamburg–Harwich	
Tor Britannia	15,794/75	Gothenburg/Esbjerg–Harwich	
Tor Scandinavia	15,673/76	Gothenburg/Esbjerg–Harwich	
Venus†	9,499/66	Gothenburg/Esbjerg–North Shields Summer charter from Fred Olsen In Winter: cruises as Black Prince	
Winston Churchill	8,658/67	Esbjerg–North Shields (for summer '85)	
Emeraude Ferries (Vedettes Blanches et Vertes)			
Solidor	907/65	Saint Malo–Jersey	ex-Langeland
Fred Olsen Line			
Braemar	14,330/80	Kristiansand–Harwich	Summer only; ex-Viking Song
Irish Continental Line			
Saint Killian II	10,256/73	Rosslare/Cork–Le Havre/Cherbourg	ex-Stena Scandinavica/ ex-Saint Killian
Saint Patrick II	7,984/73	Rosslare/Cork–Le Havre/Cherbourg	ex-Aurella

Name (†denotes on charter)	Gross tonnage/Year	Route	Former name(s) (earliest listed first)/ Notes

Isle of Man Steam Packet Co

Lady of Mann	2,990/76	Douglas summer services to Dublin, Belfast, Ardrossan and Fleetwood	
Manx Viking†	3,589/76	Douglas–Heysham	ex-*Monte Castillo*
Mona's Isle	4,657/66	Douglas–Heysham	ex-*Free Enterprise III*/ ex-*Tamira*
Mona's Queen	2,998/72	Douglas summer services to Dublin, Belfast, Ardrossan and Fleetwood	
Peveril	1,976/71	on charter 4/85 to Belfast Freight Ferries	ex-*Holmia*/ ex-*ASD Meteor*/ ex-*Penda*/ ex-*NF Jaguar*

Norfolk Line (a subsidiary of Maersk Line)

Duchess of Holland	758/69	ro-ro service Scheveningen–Great Yarmouth	
Duke of Holland II	1,596/81	ro-ro service Scheveningen–Great Yarmouth	
Duke of Norfolk	948/72	ro-ro service Scheveningen–Great Yarmouth	

North Sea Ferries

Norland	12,988/74	Hull–Rotterdam (Europoort)	
Norstar	12,502/74	Rotterdam–Hull	
Norwave	3,540/65	Hull–Zeebrugge	
Norwind	3,692/66	Zeebrugge–Hull	
new building	c.31,000/87	Hull–Rotterdam (Europoort)	
new building	c.31,000/87	Rotterdam–Hull	

Norway Line

Jupiter†	9,499/66	Bergen–Stavanger–North Shields summer only.	In winter cruises as *Black Watch* for Fred Olsen Line

Olau Line

Olau Brittania	14,990/82	Flushing–Sheerness	
Olau Hollandia	14,990/82	Flushing–Sheerness	
The Viking	4,371/74	Dunkirk West–Ramsgate	ex-*Kalle III*
Viking 6	5,216/67	Dunkirk West–Ramsgate	ex-*Stena Britannica*, ex-*Wickersham*, ex-*Viking 6*, ex-*Goelo*, ex-*Viking 6*, ex-*Sol Olympia*, *Sun Express*.

Sealink British Ferries

Antrim Princess*	3,630/67	Stranraer–Larne	
Cambridge Ferry	3,062/63	Harwich–Zeebrugge	train ferry
Darnia†	2,807/77	Stranraer–Larne	ex-*Stena Topper*
Earl Godwin	3,999/66	Weymouth–Jersey/Guernsey	ex-*Svea Drott*
Earl Granville	4,478/73	Portsmouth–Jersey/Guernsey/Cherbourg	ex-*Viking 4*
Earl Harold	3,751/71	Weymouth–Jersey/Guernsey	ex-*Ailsa Princess*
Earl William	3,765/64	Portsmouth–Jersey/Guernsey/Cherbourg	ex-*Viking II*
Galloway Princess	6,268/80	Stranraer–Larne	
Hengist	5,590/72	Folkestone–Boulogne	
Horsa	5,590/72	Folkestone–Boulogne	
Speedlink Vanguard†	3,320/73	Harwich–Zeebrugge	train ferry ex-*Stena Shipper*

*to be renamed when transferred to Heysham–Douglas

Name (†denotes on charter)	Gross tonnage/Year	Route	Former name(s) (earliest listed first)/ Notes
St Anselm	7,405/80	Dover–Calais	
St Brendan	5,426/75	Fishguard–Rosslare	ex-Stena Normandica
St Christopher	7,399/81	Dover–Calais	
St Columba	7,836/77	Holyhead–Dun Laoghaire	
St David	7,179/81	Dover–Ostend	
St Nicholas	17,043/82	Harwich–Hook of Holland	ex-Princessan Birgitta
Vortigern	4,797/69	Folkestone–Boulogne	
new building	/87	Dover–Calais	(5/85 not yet ordered)
new building	/87	Dover–Calais	

Sealink ALA (a subsidiary of Sealink British Ferries)
Saint Eloi	4,648/75	Dunkirk West–Dover	train ferry

Sealink RMT
Prins Albert	6,112/78	Ostend–Dover	
Prince Laurent	5,052/74	Ostend–Dover	
Prinses Maria Esmeralda	5,635/75	Ostend–Dover	stretched 1985
Princesse Marie Christine	5,635/76	Ostend–Dover	stretched 1986
Prinses Paola	4,356/66	Ostend–Dover summer only	passenger only ship
Prins Philippe	5,071/73	Ostend–Dover	relief ship
Reine Astrid	5,429/75	Ostend–Dover	ex-Stena Nordica/ ex-Hellas/ ex-Stena Nordica/ ex-Hellas/ ex-Stena Nordica/ ex-Stena Nautica
Stena Nautica†	6,528/74	Ostend–Dover (until 6/86)	ex-Stena Danica/ ex-Stena Nordica

Sealink SNCF
Champs Elysees	9,069/84	Calais–Dover	
Chantilly	3,400/66	Calais–Dover	
Chartres	4,586/74	Dieppe–Newhaven	
Cornouailles†	3,382/77	Dieppe–Newhaven	
Cote d'Azur	8,479/81	Calais–Dover	
Saint-Germain	3,492/51	Dunkirk West–Dover	train ferry
Senlac	5,590/73	Dieppe–Newhaven	French flag as from 2/85

Sealink SMZ
Prinses Beatrix *	9,238/78	Hook of Holland–Harwich	
Zeeland†	6,801/73	Hook of Holland–Harwich	ex-Peter Wessel
Koningin Beatrix	c.30,000/86	Hook of Holland–Harwich	(to replace both other ships)

* sold to Brittany Ferries

Smyril Line
Norrona	7,457/73	Torshavn (Faroes)–Lerwick (Shetland)– Bergen (Norway)–Hanstholm (Denmark)– Seydisfjordur (Iceland) summer only	ex-Gustav Vasa

Townsend-Thoresen Ferries
Baltic Ferry	6,455/78	Felixstowe–Rotterdam (Europort)	ro-ro vessel ex-Stena Transporter/ ex-Finnrose/ ex-Stena Transporter
Dragon ex-P&O Ferries	6,141/67	Portsmouth–Le Havre	
Gaelic Ferry	3,316/62	Portsmouth–Le Havre (summer)	ro-ro vessel
European Clearway	3,335/75	Dover–Zeebrugge	ro-ro vessel
European Enterprise	3,367/78	Dover–Zeebrugge	ro-ro vessel

Name (†denotes on charter)	Gross tonnage/Year	Route	Former name(s) (earliest listed first)/ Notes
European Trader	3,335/75	Dover–Zeebrugge	ro-ro vessel
Europic Ferry	4,190/67	Cairnryan–Larne	ro-ro vessel
Free Enterprise IV	5,049/69	Cairnryan–Larne	
Free Enterprise V	5,044/70	Dover–Zeebrugge 1985	
Free Enterprise VI	4,981/72	Dover–Zeebrugge	to be stretched 1985–86
Free Enterprise VII	4,981/73	Dover–Zeebrugge	
Free Enterprise VIII	5,169/74	Dover–Zeebrugge	
Herald of Free Enterprise	7,950/80	Dover–Calais	
Leopard ex-P&O Ferries	6,014/67	Le Havre–Portsmouth	
Nordic Ferry	6,455/78	Felixstowe–Rotterdam (Europort)	ro-ro vessel ex-Merzario Hispania/ ex-Merzario Espania
n.f. Panther ex-P&O Ferries	4,045/72	Dover–Boulogne	ex-Djursland/ex-Lasse II
Pride of Free Enterprise	7,950/80	Dover–Calais	
Spirit of Free Enterprise	7,950/79	Dover–Calais	
n.f. Tiger ex-P&O Ferries	4,045/72	Dover–Boulogne	ex-Kattegat
Viking Trader†	3,765/76	Portsmouth–Le Havre	ro-ro vessel ex-Stena Tender/ ex-Goya/ ex-Federal Nova/ ex-Caribbean Sky/ ex-Manaure VIII/ ex-Oyster Bay
Viking Valiant	6,386/75	Portsmouth–Cherbourg/Le Havre	to be stretched 1986
Viking Venturer	6,386/75	Portsmouth–Cherbourg/Le Havre	
Viking Viscount	6,386/75	Felixstowe–Zeebrugge	
Viking Voyager	6,386/75	Felixstowe–Zeebrugge	

An unusual view taken from the top of the *Earl William's* bridge as she goes astern towards the St Peter Port link-span at Guernsey en route from Jersey to Portsmouth in August 1980. *John F. Hendy*

Appendix 2

Vessels mentioned in the text and presently engaged in services within the British Isles.

(Note that some of the smaller companies listed operate more than just the vessels mentioned).

Name (†denotes on charter)	Gross tonnage/Year	Route	Former name(s) (earliest listed first)/ Notes
Blue Funnel Cruises			
Princessa	48/21	Cruises from Southampton (Town Quay)	
Caledonian MacBrayne			
Larger units			
Caledonia	1,157/66	Oban–Craignure (Mull) summer	ex-Stena Baltica
Claymore	1,631/78	Oban–Castlebay (Barra)/Lochboisdale (S. Uist) plus Oban–Coll/Tiree in winter	
Columba	1,420/64	Oban–Coll/Tiree, Colonsay, Iona cruise in summer	
Glen Sannox	1,269/57	Oban–Craignure (Mull) & Colonsay in winter	
Hebrides	1,420/64	Uig (Skye)–Tarbert (Harris)–Lochmaddy (N. Uist)	
Iona	1,324/70	Kennacraig–Port Ellen/Port Askaig (Islay)	
Isle of Arran	3,296/84	Ardrossan–Brodick (Arran)	
Juno	854/74	Gourock–Dunoon/Kilcreggan	
Jupiter	849/74	Relief ship at Gourock, Wemyss Bay	
Pioneer	1,071/74	Mallaig–Armadale (Skye) in summer	
Saturn	851/77	Wemyss Bay–Rothesay (Bute)	
Suilven	1,908/74	Ullapool–Stornoway (Lewis)	
new building	/85	to replace Hebrides at Uig	
Smaller units			
Broadford	64/66	Colintraive–Rhubodach (Bute)	
Bruernish	69/73	Tayinloan–Gigha	
Canna	69/75	Lochaline–Fishnish (Mull)	
Coll	69/73	spare 'Island' class vessel – relieves sisters	
Eigg	69/75	Oban–Lismore Island	
Isle of Cumbrae	201/77	Largs–Cumbrae slip (Cumbrae)	
Keppel	214/61	Largs–Millport in summer	ex-Rose
Kilbrannan	64/72	Scalpay–Kyles Scalpay (Harris)	
Kyleakin	225/70	Kyle of Lochalsh–Kyleakin (Skye)	
Lochalsh	225/71	Kyle of Lochalsh–Kyleakin (Skye)	
Lochmor	189/79	Mallaig–Small Isles/Kyle of Lochalsh and cruising in summer. Small Isles/Armadale in winter	
Morvern	64/73	Fionnphort (Mull) – Iona and tendering to Columba	
Portree	65/65	Colintraive–Rhubodach (Bute)	
Raasay	69/76	Sconser (Skye)–Raasay	
Rhum	69/73	Lochranza (Arran)–Claonaig	
Clyde Marine Motor Co			
Kenilworth	44/36	Gourock–Kilcreggan (year round) & Helensburgh (summer)	
The Second Snark	45/38	Relief sailings and charter work	ex-Hotspur II

Dart Pleasure Craft

Adrian Gilbert	35/57	Dartmouth–Kingswear	

Highland Regional Council

Maid of Glencoul	167/75	Corran–Ardgour	
Rosehaugh	150/67	Corran–Ardgour	

Isles of Scilly Steamship Co

Scillonian III	1,255/77	Penzance–St Mary's (Isles of Scilly)	
Tean	21/41	St Mary's–Tresco and other islands	

King Harry Steam Ferry Co

King Harry Ferry	—/74	Chain ferry service across the River Fal	

Merseyside Passenger Transport Executive

Mountwood	464/60	Liverpool–Woodside/Seacombe	
Overchurch	468/62	Liverpool–Woodside/Seacombe	
Royal Iris	1,234/51	Ferry services (as above), cruises and restaurant use	
Woodchurch	462/60	Liverpool–Woodside/Seacombe	

Note: Ferry services to International Garden Festival site at Otterspool continue in 1985.

Millbrook Steamboat & Trading Co

Edgcumbe Belle	35/57	Cruises around Plymouth Docks and Drake Island ferry	ex-Humphrey Gilbert
Northern Belle	/29	Stonehouse–Cremyll	

Norse Atlantic Ferries trading as **Viking Island Ferries**

Syllingar	921/56	Kirkwall (Orkney)–Pierowall (Westray)–Scalloway (Shetland)	ex-Scillonian/ex-Devonia/ ex-Devoniun

Alan Oliver

Wyre Lady	38/38	Waterbus service on Sheffield & South Yorkshire Navigation.	ex-Ashton/ex-Gourockian

Orkney Islands Shipping Co

Clytus	30/44	Services from Kirkwall–Eday–Stronsay–Sanday– Papa Westray–Westray–Rousay–Egilsay–Wyre–	
Hoy Head	94/55	North Ronaldsay–Shapinsay worked by Clytus, Islander and Orcadia.	
Islander (cargo ship)	250/69	Stromness and Houton to Graemsay, Hoy and Flotta worked by Hoy Head and car ferry Lyrawa Bay	
Lyrawa Bay	102/70		(ex-Sam)
Orcadia	619/62		

Orwell & Harwich Navigation Co

Brightlingsea	51/25	Harwich–Felixstowe and cruising	

Paddle Steam Navigation Ltd

Kingswear Castle	94/24	Preserved paddle steamer from the River Dart. Now cruises during summer week-ends on River Medway	

P&O Ferries (Orkney & Shetland services)

ROF Beaver	983/71	ro-ro service between Leith–Lerwick (Shetland)	ex-Bibiana/ex-Irish Famel/ ex-Monarch Famel/ ex-Bibiana/ex-Helga I
St Clair	4,468/65	Aberdeen–Lerwick (Shetland)	ex-Peter Pan/ ex-SF Panther/ex-Terje Vigen
St Magnus	1,206/70	Lerwick–Stromness–Aberdeen	ex-Donautal/ ex-Ulster Sportsman/ex-Dorset
St Ola	1,345/75	Scrabster–Stromness (Orkney)	

Philip & Son

Dartmouth/Kingswear

Higher Ferry	—/60	Higher ferry on the River Dart	

Portsmouth Harbour Ferry Co

Gosport Queen	159/66	Portsmouth–Gosport	
Portsmouth Queen	159/66	Portsmouth–Gosport	
Solent Enterprise	274/71	relief ferry and cruises	ex-Gay Enterprise

Sealink British Ferries

Brading	986/48	Portsmouth–Ryde (Isle of Wight)	
Caedmon	764/73	Lymington–Yarmouth (Isle of Wight)	
Cenred	761/73	Lymington–Yarmouth	
Cenwulf	761/73	Lymington–Yarmouth	
Cuthred	704/69	Portsmouth–Fishbourne (Isle of Wight)	
Edith	214/61	Gravesend–Tilbury	
Southsea	986/48	Portsmouth–Ryde	
St Catherine	2,036/83	Portsmouth–Fishbourne	
St Helen	2,036/83	Portsmouth–Fishbourne	
new building	c.2,000/86	Portsmouth–Fishbourne	

Shetland Islands Council

Filla	131/83	Out Skerries–Lerwick (Mainland)	
Fivla	/85	Gutcher (Yell)–Belmont (Unst)–Oddsta (Fetlar)	
Fylga	147/74	Toft (Mainland)–Ulsta (Yell)	
Geira	147/73	for sale – replaced by Fivla	
Grima	147/73	Lerwick (Mainland)–Maryfield (Bressay)	
Hendra	225/82	Laxo (Mainland)–Symbister (Whalsay)	
Kjella	158/57	reserve ship	
Thora	147/75	Toft (Mainland)–Ulsta (Yell)	

Southern Coastcrafts

Hotspur IV	50/46	Hythe–Southampton	
Hythe Hotspur	119/74	Hythe–Southampton and cruises	ex-Southsea Queen
New Forester	49/82	Hythe–Southampton and cruises	

Southampton, Isle of Wight & South of England Royal Mail Steam Packet Co, trading as **Red Funnel Services**

Cowes Castle	912/65	Southampton-Cowes/East Cowes (Isle of Wight)	
Netley Castle	1,183/74	Southampton–Cowes/East Cowes	
Norris Castle	922/68	Southampton–Cowes/East Cowes	

South Hams District Council

Dartmouth Ferry Float II	28/47	Lower ferry on River Dart between Kingswear–	
Dartmouth Ferry Float III	31/58	Dartmouth. Both propelled by small tugs	

Strathclyde Regional Council

Renfrew Rose	/84	Renfrew–Yoker	
Yoker Swan	/84	Renfrew–Yoker	

C. Toms & Son

No 3	/63	Fowey–Bodinnick ferry across the River Fowey.	
No 4	/75	Both floats are powered by small launches	

Torpoint Ferry

1	/60	Torpoint–Devonport chain ferries across the	
2	/61	River Tamar	
3	/68		

Tyne and Wear Passenger Transport Executive

Shieldsman	93/76	North Shields–South Shields	

Name (†denotes on charter)	Gross tonnage/Year	Route	Former name(s) (earliest listed first)/ Notes
Waverley Steam Navigation Co			
Waverley	693/47	Preserved paddle steamer based on Glasgow but also seen in Bristol Channel, Solent and Thames areas	
Western Isles Islands Council			
Eilean Bhearnaraigh	69/83	Newton (N. Uist)–Berneray	
Eilean Na H-Oige	69/80	Ludaig (S. Uist)–Eriskay	
Western Ferries (Clyde) Ltd			
Sound of Gigha	65/66	Port Askaig (Islay)–Feolin (Jura)	ex-Isle of Gigha
Sound of Sanda	275/38	Hunter's Quay–McInroy's Point	ex-Lymington
Sound of Scarba	175/60	Hunter's Quay–McInroy's Point	ex-Olandssund III
Sound of Shuna	244/62	Hunter's Quay–McInroy's Point	ex-Olandssund IV

Appendix 3

High Speed Craft

Name (†denotes on charter)	Gross tonnage/Year	Route	Former name(s) (earliest listed first)/ Notes
Condor Ltd (hydrofoils)			
Condor 4	129/74	Saint Malo–Jersey/Guernsey/Sark & Alderney	
Condor 5	174/76	services not operated during winter months	
Condor 7	/85		
Hoverspeed		Dover–Boulogne/Calais	
Sir Christopher (GH 2008)	/72		former Hoverlloyd SRN 4 Mk II
Sure (GH 2005)	/69		former Hoverlloyd SRN 4 Mk II
Swift (GH 2004)	/69		former Hoverlloyd SRN 4 Mk II
The Prince of Wales GH 2054	/77		former Hoverlloyd SRN 4 Mk II
The Princess Anne GH 2001	/69		former Seaspeed SRN 4 Mk III
The Princess Margaret GH 2006	/68		former Seaspeed SRN 4 Mk III
Hovertravel			
Resolution (GH 2088)	/83	Ryde–Southsea	AP1-88 hovercraft
Tenacity (GH 2087)	/83	Ryde–Southsea	AP1-88 hovercraft
Red Funnel Services (hydrofoils)			
Shearwater 3	62/72		
Shearwater 4	62/73	Southampton–Cowes	
Shearwater 5	62/80		
Shearwater 6	62/82		

Sealink British Ferries

new building	/86	Portsmouth–Ryde	catamaran ferries
new building	/86	Portsmouth–Ryde	to replace the 1948 passenger ships. (first ordered 5/85)

Sealink RMT

Princesse Clementine	289/81	Ostend–Dover	Boeing jetfoil craft
Prinses Stephanie	289/81	Ostend–Dover	Boeing jetfoil craft

Torbay Seaways (hydrofoil)

Star Capricorn	135/67	Torquay–Alderney–Guernsey–Jersey (summer only)	ex-*Springeren*

Vedettes Armoricaines

Jaguar	245/79	Saint Malo–Jersey (summer only)

Vedettes Blanches et Vertes

Belle de Dinard	195/72	Granville–Jersey	Westermarin catamaran ex-*Karmsund*
Trident	252/82	Saint Malo–Jersey (both summer services)	Westermarin catamaran

Below:
Princesse Clementine   John F. Hendy